Intellectual Property and the New Global Japanese Economy

This book examines how intellectual property (IP) is used in Japan, and how in recent years Japan has developed a new approach to IP, which stresses the importance of innovation, in order to rescue the Japanese economy from the stagnation and deflation that characterized the 1990s. It shows how the Japanese economy revitalized itself during the Koizumi administration of 2001–2006 using structural reform both economically and politically, as well as a radical IP drive that both embraced the Japanese population at large and integrated Japan into the global economy. It discusses landmark decisions involving employees' rights to compensation and a bold attempt by the Tokyo Stock Exchange to create a market in cooperation with the London Stock Exchange that caters to small and medium-sized enterprises (SMEs), which are often the locus of innovation, all of which points to a period of change that had only previously occurred in the nineteenth century. Overall, this book, which incorporates information provided by frontline decision makers in Japan, is essential reading for all those interested in understanding the modern Japanese economy, the new role of IP in revitalizing the economy and how Japan is adapting to exploit the opportunities and challenges of an increasingly globalized world.

Ruth Taplin is the author/editor of over 200 articles and 14 books. The most recent are: *Exploiting Patent Rights and a New Climate for Innovation in Japan*; *Japanese Decision Making* (reprinted by Routledge, 2005); *Valuing Intellectual Property in Japan, Britain and the United States*; *Risk Management and Innovation in Japan, Britain and the United States*; *Japanese Telecommunications: Market and Policy in Transition*; *Innovation and Business Partnering in Japan, Europe and the United States* and *Outsourcing and Human Resource Management: An International Survey* (the last five also published by Routledge). Professor Taplin has been editor of the *Journal of Interdisciplinary Economics* for 15 years. She is Director of the Center for Japanese and East Asian Studies, which won Exporter of the Year in Trading/Pathfinder in 2000 for the UK. Currently she is a Research Fellow at Birkbeck College, University of London and at the University of Leicester, and has been a Visiting Professor and Research Fellow at a number of universities in the UK and abroad.

Routledge Studies in the Growth Economies of Asia

1. **The Changing Capital Markets of East Asia**
   Edited by Ky Cao

2. **Financial Reform in China**
   Edited by On Kit Tam

3. **Women and Industrialization in Asia**
   Edited by Susan Horton

4. **Japan's Trade Policy**
   Action or reaction?
   Yumiko Mikanagi

5. **The Japanese Election System**
   Three analytical perspectives
   Junichiro Wada

6. **The Economics of the Latecomers**
   Catching-up, technology transfer and institutions in Germany, Japan and South Korea
   Jang-Sup Shin

7. **Industrialization in Malaysia**
   Import substitution and infant industry performance
   Rokiah Alavi

8. **Economic Development in Twentieth Century East Asia**
   The international context
   Edited by Aiko Ikeo

9. **The Politics of Economic Development in Indonesia**
   Contending perspectives
   Edited by Ian Chalmers and Vedi R. Hadiz

10. **Studies in the Economic History of the Pacific Rim**
    Edited by Sally M. Miller, A. J. H. Latham and Dennis O. Flynn

11. **Workers and the State in New Order Indonesia**
    Vedi R. Hadiz

12. **The Japanese Foreign Exchange Market**
    Beate Reszat

13. **Exchange Rate Policies in Emerging Asian Countries**
    Edited by Stefan Collignon, Jean Pisani-Ferry and Yung Chul Park

14. **Chinese Firms and Technology in the Reform Era**
    Yizheng Shi

15. **Japanese Views on Economic Development**
    Diverse paths to the market
    Kenichi Ohno and Izumi Ohno

16. **Technological Capabilities and Export Success in Asia**
    Edited by Dieter Ernst, Tom Ganiatsos and Lynn Mytelka

17. **Trade and Investment in China**
    The European experience
    Edited by Roger Strange, Jim Slater and Limin Wang

18. **Technology and Innovation in Japan**
    Policy and management for the twenty-first century
    Edited by Martin Hemmert and Christian Oberländer

19. **Trade Policy Issues in Asian Development**
    Prema-chandra Athukorala

20. **Economic Integration in the Asia Pacific Region**
    Ippei Yamazawa

21. **Japan's War Economy**
    Edited by Erich Pauer

22. **Industrial Technology Development in Malaysia**
    Industry and firm studies
    Edited by Jomo K. S., Greg Felker and Rajah Rasiah

23. **Technology, Competitiveness and the State**
    Malaysia's industrial technology policies
    Edited by Jomo K. S. and Greg Felker

24. **Corporatism and Korean Capitalism**
    Edited by Dennis L. McNamara

25. **Japanese Science**
    Samuel Coleman

26. **Capital and Labour in Japan**
    The functions of two factor markets
    Toshiaki Tachibanaki and Atsuhiro Taki

27. **Asia Pacific Dynamism 1550–2000**
    Edited by A. J. H. Latham and Heita Kawakatsu

28. **The Political Economy of Development and Environment in Korea**
    Jae-Yong Chung and Richard J. Kirkby

29 **Japanese Economics and Economists since 1945**
    Edited by Aiko Ikeo

30 **China's Entry into the World Trade Organisation**
    Edited by Peter Drysdale and Ligang Song

31 **Hong Kong as an International Financial Centre**
    Emergence and development 1945–1965
    Catherine R. Schenk

32 **Impediments to Trade in Services**
    Measurement and policy implication
    Edited by Christopher Findlay and Tony Warren

    The Japanese Industrial Economy
    Late development and cultural causation
    Ian Inkster

34 **China and the Long March to Global Trade**
    The accession of China to the World Trade Organization
    Edited by Alan S. Alexandroff, Sylvia Ostry and Rafael Gomez

35 **Capitalist Development and Economism in East Asia**
    The rise of Hong Kong, Singapore, Taiwan, and South Korea
    Kui-Wai Li

36 **Women and Work in Globalizing Asia**
    Edited by Dong-Sook S. Gills and Nicola Piper

37 **Financial Markets and Policies in East Asia**
    Gordon de Brouwer

38 **Developmentalism and Dependency in Southeast Asia**
    The case of the automotive industry
    Jason P. Abbott

39 **Law and Labour Market Regulation in East Asia**
    Edited by Sean Cooney, Tim Lindsey, Richard Mitchell and Ying Zhu

40 **The Economy of the Philippines**
    Elites, inequalities and economic restructuring
    Peter Krinks

41 **China's Third Economic Transformation**
    The rise of the private economy
    Edited by Ross Garnaut and Ligang Song

42 **The Vietnamese Economy**
    Awakening the dormant dragon
    Edited by Binh Tran-Nam and Chi Do Pham

43 **Restructuring Korea Inc.**
    Jang-Sup Shin and Ha-Joon Chang

44 **Development and Structural Change in the Asia-Pacific**
    Globalising miracles or end of a model?
    Edited by Martin Andersson and Christer Gunnarsson

45 **State Collaboration and Development Strategies in China**
    The case of the China–Singapore Suzhou Industrial Park (1992–2002)
    Alexius Pereira

46 **Capital and Knowledge in Asia**
    Changing power relations
    Edited by Heidi Dahles and Otto van den Muijzenberg

47 **Southeast Asian Paper Tigers?**
    From miracle to debacle and beyond
    Edited by Jomo K. S.

48 **Manufacturing Competitiveness in Asia**
    How internationally competitive national firms and industries developed in East Asia
    Edited by Jomo K. S.

49 **The Korean Economy at the Crossroads**
    Edited by MoonJoong Tcha and Chung-Sok Suh

50 **Ethnic Business**
    Chinese capitalism in Southeast Asia
    Edited by Jomo K. S. and Brian C. Folk

51 **Exchange Rate Regimes in East Asia**
    Edited by Gordon de Brouwer and Masahiro Kawai

52 **Financial Governance in East Asia**
    Policy dialogue, surveillance and cooperation
    Edited by Gordon de Brouwer and Yunjong Wang

53 **Designing Financial Systems in East Asia and Japan**
    Edited by Joseph P. H. Fan, Masaharu Hanazaki and Juro Teranishi

54 **State Competence and Economic Growth in Japan**
    Yoshiro Miwa

55 **Understanding Japanese Saving**
    Does population aging matter?
    Robert Dekle

56 **The Rise and Fall of the East Asian Growth System, 1951–2000**
    International competitiveness and rapid economic growth
    Xiaoming Huang

57 **Service Industries and Asia-Pacific Cities**
New development trajectories
Edited by P. W. Daniels, K. C. Ho and T. A. Hutton

58 **Unemployment in Asia**
Edited by John Benson and Ying Zhu

59 **Risk Management and Innovation in Japan, Britain and the United States**
Edited by Ruth Taplin

60 **Japan's Development Aid to China**
The long-running foreign policy of engagement
Tsukasa Takamine

61 **Chinese Capitalism and the Modernist Vision**
Satyananda J. Gabriel

62 **Japanese Telecommunications**
Market and policy in transition
Edited by Ruth Taplin and Masako Wakui

63 **East Asia, Globalization and the New Economy**
F. Gerard Adams

64 **China as a World Factory**
Edited by Kevin Honglin Zhang

65 **China's State Owned Enterprise Reforms**
An industrial and CEO approach
Juan Antonio Fernandez and Leila Fernandez-Stembridge

66 **China and India**
A tale of two economies
Dilip K. Das

67 **Innovation and Business Partnering in Japan, Europe and the United States**
Edited by Ruth Taplin

68 **Asian Informal Workers**
Global risks local protection
Santosh Mehrotra and Mario Biggeri

69 **The Rise of the Corporate Economy in Southeast Asia**
Rajeswary Ampalavanar Brown

70 **The Singapore Economy**
An econometric perspective
Tilak Abeyshinge and Keen Meng Choy

71 **A Basket Currency for Asia**
Edited by Takatoshi Ito

72 **Private Enterprises and China's Economic Development**
Edited by Shuanglin Lin and Xiaodong Zhu

73 **The Korean Developmental State**
From dirigisme to neo-liberalism
Iain Pirie

74 **Accelerating Japan's Economic Growth**
Resolving Japan's growth controversy
Edited by F. Gerard Adams, Lawrence R. Klein, Yuzo Kumasaka and Akihiko Shinozaki

75 **China's Emergent Political Economy**
Capitalism in the dragon's lair
Edited by Christopher A. McNally

76 **The Political Economy of the SARS Epidemic**
The impact on human resources in East Asia
Grace O. M. Lee and Malcolm Warner

77 **India's Emerging Financial Market**
A flow of funds model
Tomoe Moore

78 **Outsourcing and Human Resource Management**
An international survey
Edited by Ruth Taplin

79 **Globalization, Labor Markets and Inequality in India**
Dipak Mazumdar and Sandip Sarkar

80 **Globalization and the Indian Economy**
Roadmap to a convertible rupee
Satyendra S. Nayak

81 **Economic Cooperation between Singapore and India**
An alliance in the making
Faizal Yahya

82 **The United States and the Malaysian Economy**
Shakila Yacob

83 **Banking Reform in Southeast Asia**
The region's decisive decade
Malcolm Cook

84 **Trade Unions in Asia**
An economic and sociological analysis
Edited by John Benson and Ying Zhu

85 **Trade Liberalisation and Regional Disparity in Pakistan**
Muhammad Shoaib Butt and Jayatilleke S. Bandara

86 **Financial Development and Economic Growth in Malaysia**
James Ang

87 **Intellectual Property and the New Global Japanese Economy**
Ruth Taplin

Intellectual Property and the New Global Japanese Economy

Ruth Taplin

Routledge
Taylor & Francis Group

LONDON AND NEW YORK

First published 2009
by Routledge
2 Park Square, Milton Park, Abingdon, Oxon OX14 4RN

Simultaneously published in the USA and Canada
by Routledge
270 Madison Avenue, New York, NY 10016

Routledge is an imprint of the Taylor & Francis Group, an informa business

© 2009 Ruth Taplin

Typeset in Times New Roman by
Florence Production Ltd, Stoodleigh, Devon
Printed and bound in the UK by the
MPG Books Group

All rights reserved. No part of this book may be reprinted or
reproduced or utilized in any form or by any electronic, mechanical,
or other means, now known or hereafter invented, including photocopying
and recording, or in any information storage or retrieval system,
without permission in writing from the publishers.

British Library Cataloguing in Publication Data
A catalogue record for this book is available from the British Library

Library of Congress Cataloging in Publication Data
Taplin, Ruth.
　Intellectual property and the new global Japanese economy/Ruth Taplin.
　　p. cm. – (Routledge studies in the growth economies of Asia)
　Includes bibliographical references and index.
　1. Intellectual property – Economic aspects – Japan. 2. Japan –
Economic policy – 1989–. I. Title.
KNX1155.T366 2009
346.5204′8–dc22   2008040873

ISBN10: 0–415–46597–4 (hbk)
ISBN10: 0–203–88029–3 (ebk)

ISBN13: 978–0–415–46597–7 (hbk)
ISBN13: 978–0–203–88029–6 (ebk)

The author would like to dedicate this book to Sir Nicholas Pumfrey, Lord Justice of Appeal, whose untimely death last Christmas Eve was a cause of great sadness to those in the field of Intellectual Property. The author was much indebted to his incisive comments concerning her book, *Valuing Intellectual Property in Japan, Britain and the United States*.

Contents

List of figures		xi
Acknowledgements		xiii
List of abbreviations		xv
List of Japanese terms		xvii
1	Roots of the IP drive and economic globalization	1
2	Japan as an IP nation	17
3	Historical perspectives of the economy and IP	27
4	Cross-border IP and the fast-tracking of patent applications	39
5	Changes to the Patent Court and employees' rights to compensation	56
6	Changes in Japanese corporate governance	68
7	Future developments in the Japanese exchanges	81
8	Conclusion	94
	Appendix	107
	Notes	135
	Index	141

Figures

4.1 The number of cases for IPR (First Instance, Tokyo District Court) and the average length required for inquiry   47
7.1 Average trading value per company   84

PowerPoint slides are from pages 108 to 133.

Acknowledgements

The author would like to thank the following sponsors, colleagues and contributors for their valuable assistance with this book. Sponsors include the Great Britain Sasakawa Foundation, which has shown great support in sponsoring her books over the years; Mr Tokumine, owner of the Japan Centre, who has also offered continued support; Nomura International London and its Chairman, Lord Marshall, whom the author knows from CBI days; and the Nomura Foundation of Japan, which awarded her a grant to further her research while in Japan in July 2007. She is also grateful to JAL for helping to sponsor her flights to Japan, and to Osaka City University for being her research host for many years.

Invaluable contributions have been made to a much required further understanding of Japanese corporate governance, history and business. Thanks go to Professor Nishizawa Akio of Tohoku University; Professor Takahashi Eiji of Osaka City University; and Professor Murakami Hiroshi of Kanazawa University.

For the invaluable material concerning intellectual property and employee rights to compensation, and for his continued support, great thanks go to Judge Shitara Ryuichi, Judge of the Tokyo District Court.

Abbreviations

AIM	Alternative Investment Market
AIPLA	American Intellectual Property Law Association
AIST	National Institute of Advanced Industrial Science and Technology (formerly Agency of Industrial Science and Technology)
ASBJ	Accounting Standards Board of Japan
ASEAN	Association of South East Asian Nations
AUTM	Association of University Technical Managers
BOJ	Bank of Japan
CEFP	Council on Economic and Fiscal Policy
CPI	Consumer Price Index
DBJ	Development Bank of Japan
DPJ	Democratic Party of Japan
EPO	European Patent Office
FDA	Food and Drug Administration
FDI	foreign direct investment
GAAP	generally accepted accounting principle
GDP	gross domestic product
IASB	International Accounting Standards Board
IFRS	International Financial Reporting Standard
IP	intellectual property
IPO	initial public offering
IPR	intellectual property rights
IT	information technology
JICA	Japan International Cooperation Agency
JIII	Japanese Institute for Inventions and Innovation
JPAA	Japan Patent Attorneys Association
JPIO	Japanese Patent Information Organization
JPO	Japan Patent Office

J-SOX	Japan's Financial Instruments and Exchange Law
KIPO	Korean Intellectual Property Office
LDP	Liberal Democratic Party
LED	light-emitting diode
LSE	London Stock Exchange
M&A	mergers and acquisitions
MEXT	Ministry of Education, Sport, Science and Technology
Mothers	market of the high-growth and emerging stocks
NEET	not in education, employment or training
NPIT	National Centre of Industrial Property Information
NPL	non-performing loan
ODA	Orphan Drug Act
OFF	office of first filing
OSF	office of second filing
P&A	purchase and assumption
PFI	private finance initiative
PPH	patent prosecution highway
R&D	research and development
SMEs	small and medium-sized enterprises
SPC	special purpose company
TLO	technical licensing organization
TSE	Tokyo Stock Exchange
UKPO	United Kingdom Patent Office
USPTO	United States Patent and Trademark Office
WIPO	World Intellectual Property Organization
WTO	World Trade Organization

Japanese terms

bakufu	central government
bakuhan	the control by the *bakufu* of the land through *han* units
bengoshi	attorneys at law
benrishi	patent attorneys
bushi	knightly nobility
daimyo	feudal lord
endaka	appreciation of the yen
Fuki Benrishi	Patent Attorney with Addendum to Registration
gappei taika	countervalue
giri	reciprocal obligation
gomei kaisha	general partnership companies
goshi kaisha	limited partnership companies
han	the domains of the *daimyo* and the power structure
jito	warriors
kabu	share
kabu nakama	participation in a guild
kaisha	large companies
kanji	Chinese characters
katoku	head of *bushi* group
kawase kaisha	exchange companies
keiretsu	trading arm or subsidary of a large company
kobun	see *oyabun/kobun*
kokutai	(lit. national body/structure – a sort of mystical 'national essence')
kuge	nobles of the imperial court

menju-fukuhai	obeying one's superiors outwardly, while rebelling against them inwardly
nemawashi	preparing the ground through negotiation
oyabun/kobun	parent/child (relationship)
ryogaeya	exchange
shacho	president of a company
shachokai	meetings of company presidents
shinkabu-yoyakuken	stock acquisition rights
sho	manorial properties
shogun	sort of 'generalissimo'; the most powerful *daimyo*
sogo shosha	large non-family-owned, vertically integrated company
sokai-ya	company racketeers
tankan	investigation or exploratory
zaibatsu	large traditional, family-owned company
zoku-gin	groups affiliated with vested interests

1 Roots of the IP drive and economic globalization

A political and economic *tsunami* washes over Japan

In April 2001, Japan – the second largest economy in the world – experienced a political and economic *tsunami* that would shake the country out of its torpor for the next five years and five months. It was delivered in the form of Koizumi Junichiro, who was elected to the Presidency of the Liberal Democratic Party (LDP), subsequently to become Prime Minister of Japan. As most nations and people seek a figure of deliverance in harsh times, Prime Minister Koizumi almost became a religious-like figure who appealed directly to the people of Japan to support his radical reforms. This is unusual in a country where politicians have a more usual disdain for and remote relationship with the electorate, preferring to seek support and solace from fellow party members in their bid to hold on to power, and in a nation that is less than religious in outlook. By appealing to three million LDP members directly, he also addressed the public's need to see a reformed Japan that would become prosperous once more. Japanese people, and women in particular, resented and protested against the policies of former Prime Minister Hashimoto Ryutaro (1996–8), who had tried to raise the consumption tax. Koizumi was admired in Japan for being plain speaking and honest. This perception was aided by direct interaction through the media and meetings at town halls.

Prime Minister Koizumi came from a family of politicians and his grandfather had already tried to reform Posts and Telecommunications by splitting the two, which his grandson managed to accomplish amid great opposition. He was committed throughout his political career to structural reform that began in the 1970s, when he was parliamentary vice minister of the Ministry of Finance, while the national debt was spiralling out of control. When he was Minister of Posts and Telecommunications in the 1990s he began his struggle for reform by attempting to redirect the flow of funds from postal savings, insurance and national pensions into an alternative budget, but never succeeded. He ran for LDP president twice before he finally succeeded in 2001, as a young aggressive reformer.

Pillars of support for reform

Prime Minister Koizumi also had a talent for choosing like-minded people to support his reforms and defended them when under attack. His greatest expertise and support came from Iijima Isao, who was his chief of staff and who was skilled in recruiting reform-minded bureaucrats to support reforms and in lobbying politicians to ensure reform-based legislation was passed. He served Mr Koizumi throughout his political career as an executive and legislative aide.

Takenaka Heizo was an unusual choice – he had a Ph.D. from Hitosubashi University, had formerly worked at the Development Bank of Japan (DBJ) and was a holder of several academic posts. Dr Takenaka shared with Mr Iijima the passion for reform and the former, despite being a political novice, engaged in successful *nemawashi* (preparing the ground through negotiation) to persuade key LDP leaders and senior bureaucrats to support legislative reforms put forward by the Koizumi government.

Dr Takenaka endured a great number of political attacks, which he endured with patience and with the support of Prime Minister Koizumi, because he assisted in breaking up the close relations between LDP politicians, business executives and bureaucrats. Such close relations often culminated in wasteful projects, such as unnecessary bridge-building or other projects such as Seagaia in Miyazaki prefecture, which proved to be white elephants, but were lucrative for local bureaucrats and businessmen and were also carried out to buy rural votes. The pork-barrelling activities of corrupt politicians were high on Dr Takenaka's list to eliminate. Public corporations were privatized to make them more efficient and less corrupt and the issuance of national bonds was reduced.[1] The other pillar of Prime Minister Koizumi's reform drives was Arai Hisamitsu, who promoted vigorously and successfully the drive for Japan to be an intellectual property (IP) nation as the Secretary General of the IP Strategy Headquarters, Japanese Cabinet.

In this book we will concentrate on the economic policies of globalization and eliminating waste that occurred under the jurisdiction of Dr Takenaka and the IP reform so capably carried out by Mr Arai.

The need for economic reform

In the decade prior to 1999, the Japanese economy experienced severe recession and deflation. Banks were saddled with non-performing loans; the yen was so strong during the period of *endaka* (appreciation of the yen) in 1985 that the usual way of recovering through expanding exports globally became less of a viable option; consumers were neither spending nor saving in banks that offered miniscule or non-existent interest rates; and the property market had collapsed.

In addition to the internal stagnation were the external factors of the September 11 terrorist attacks in 2001 in the United States coupled with the continuing negative fall-out from the dotcom boom.

Corporate Japan continued in its traditional path of providing loans through *giri*, or reciprocal obligation, accruing even greater debt burdens that were never guaranteed to be repaid. Continuing with lifetime employment and other non-sustainable labour policies, in addition to retaining non-profitable, inefficient companies or parts of companies, was preventing the freeing of labour and capital to be used more productively to encourage growth.

Dr Takenaka believed that the Japanese economy could only return to a path of growth by vigorously promoting structural reform in all areas, such as deregulation, fiscal reform and the reform of both pension and insurance systems.

Measures to be taken by financial authorities

By the time the economy bottomed out in 2002, after nearly 15 years of economic uncertainty, the financial authorities had learned a number of lessons for the future and a number of structural reforms were being carried out to prevent the economic disasters of the 1990s.

The size and scale of damage wreaked on the Japanese economy during the 1990s need to be understood before the structural solutions are outlined and the lessons learned analysed. The bursting of the bubble economy and collapse of the property market in 1990 caused wide fluctuations in capital gains and losses in the Japanese corporate sector. The situation was so severe that, by 2004, total capital since the bursting of the bubble had still not recovered sufficiently.

The two characteristics of the bubble bursting in Japan were the scale of loss and the asymmetry of the loss by size and industry of the companies. Overall loses were nearly one-third of nominal gross domestic product (GDP), which was excessively high for a modern economy. The loss was even larger in small and medium-sized enterprises (SMEs). By contrast, the losses to large manufacturing companies were relatively small, while the loss of non-manufacturing SMEs has been so great that full recovery has not been achieved by 2008. The lack of symmetry as to what sectors were the most affected was largely due to commercial property being the major sector affected and non-manufacturing companies not having to compete on a global scale because they were protected by the government.

Large manufacturing companies were forced to restructure and globalize after the appreciation of the yen (*endaka*) in 1985, which had made them globally competitive and privately financed. Japanese banks eagerly – or some would argue recklessly – financed the non-manufacturing sector, most particularly the real estate industry, without checking that such industries were globally competitive and able to sustain themselves.

It was the scale and asymmetry of loss that brought about serious delays in structural reform policies that were supported by the majority of Japanese people. Ninety per cent of the labour force works for SMEs or the non-manufacturing sector, which made the seriousness of the loss even greater. Had the banks disposed of the non-performing loans (NPLs) all at once, it could have been the case that the bulk of Japanese companies would have become bankrupt, with the result that almost 90 per cent of the population would have become unemployed, which would have been a catastrophe. To prevent panic the government did not inform the Japanese people of the scale of the impending disaster, which was exacerbated by a credit crunch, because the underdevelopment of the corporate bonds and stock market through which companies could raise funds led to an increase in NPLs, accompanied by a reduction in bank profits with an increase in deficits.[2]

Structural reform programme

With the scale of economic problems at epic proportions, the Japanese economy was suffering from a cyclical downturn because of slowdown in the global economy. Industrial production and business investment declined and, in November 2001, unemployment reached an all-time post-war record of 5.5 per cent. The Koizumi government had to act quickly and efficiently and there was little room for political factional games.

The Koizumi government under Dr Takenaka introduced two economic policy packages to ease the crisis. One was the 'Advanced Reform Programme' in October 2001, which included measures for new job creation, safety nets for those who had lost their jobs and for SMEs and measures addressing the NPL problems. In December, the second package was adopted by the Koizumi government – the 'Emergency Action Programme for Structural Reform', which was to accelerate structural reforms. The Action Programme was accompanied by a second draft supplementary budget of roughly $US 34 billion, which was allocated to social infrastructure to facilitate structural reform that lifted GDP by 0.9 per cent over the next year. Instrumental to the success of these policies was the government working with the Bank of Japan (BOJ) to continue the latter's adoption of appropriate and flexible monetary policies to stem deflation.

Bank of Japan measures to deal with the financial crisis

The BOJ introduced a safety net to prevent systemic risk, which included the speedy purchase and assumption (P&A) scheme. The process meant closing a failed bank on a Friday, transferring protected deposits and sound assets to another bank during the weekend and opening the bank on the following Monday. If the risk of systemic risk was too large, as in the case of large banks becoming bankrupt, the special safety net included transferring deposits to bridge banks and public capital injection into the failed banks or simply a transitional nationalization of these banks.

In tandem with the Koizumi government, the BOJ introduced a bridge bank to take over the whole balance sheet of the failed institutions, investing 20 billion yen, for example, which had been lost.

The BOJ tried very hard to make people aware of the importance of disclosure, but it was not taken seriously as transparency had never been a feature of Japanese financial institutions. In fact, in line with the cultural tendencies of not losing face and not speaking openly of financial situations, people were not inclined to be involved in disclosure. As bankruptcies of financial institutions continued, the dire situation forced the government to produce a 'comprehensive' safety net to prevent systemic risk. The government, therefore, declared a blanket guarantee for all deposits, revised the deposit insurance law almost every year and made new legislation for the protection of the financial system.

The delay in dealing with disclosure and making the population aware of the extent of NPLs allowed the continuation of inefficient and poorly managed corporations and banks. In addition, the delay in awareness and disclosure of the NPLs resulted in the gradual disposal of losses and the construction of safety nets. The government before the Koizumi administration lacked strong leadership and could not push through the reforms that were so necessary to restore the equilibrium of the Japanese economy and bring it into positive growth.[3]

The Koizumi reforms to the economy

As Dr Takenaka pointed out, the essential strength of the Koizumi government lay with its ability to implement structural reform by fighting against vested interests. Vested interests were pulling the economy to pieces, with every interest group taking its own direction and not pulling together to fight economic instability. Instead of revitalizing the rural areas, large cumbersome projects were built with favours granted to certain construction companies and with the outcome of the projects contributing nothing to sustained growth. The projects were isolated and largely unnecessary, benefiting only a small group of people. The Japan Highway Public Corporation was a great offender in squandering public money and undertaking wasteful projects. The Koizumi administration put a stop to this by privatizing it and making it accountable. The Government Housing Loan Corporation was discontinued and expenditure on public corporations was reduced by over one trillion yen in a year.

Administrative reorganization served to make Prime Minister Koizumi more effective. He created a Council on Economic and Fiscal Policy (CEFP) in the Cabinet Office, which took a central role in the formulation of economic and fiscal policies. Dr Takenaka noted that the Council provided him with 'machines' for his leadership. The Council was comprised of economic ministers and 'wise men' from the private sector and was presided over by Prime Minister Koizumi himself. In line with this hands-on approach, Dr Takenaka steered the Council to ensure that it formed the underpinning of the Prime Minister's leadership.

Council-inspired structural reforms

In June 2001, the first year of the Koizumi government, the Council drafted a document entitled 'Basic Policies for Macroeconomic Management'. The essence of this policy document was 'no growth without reform'. To push this forward a 'Reform Schedule' was soon created, which set out a clear timetable for the 'Basic Policies' to be implemented. Another document entitled 'Reform and Prospects' set out targets for fiscal consolidation and the medium-term policy framework that focused on structural reforms. It also included a forecast for economic growth over the next decade.

One of the first economic goals was to defeat deflation, which was undermining economic fundamentals and health. Their target was a 2 per cent growth rate over the next decade.

Strategy for non-performing loans

The 'Reform Schedule' included a set of measures to accelerate the disposal of NPLs and revitalize the financial sector. The Japanese Financial Services Authority introduced a number of special inspections to ensure adequate loan classification and to secure enough loan loss provision. The DBJ, for whom Dr Takenaka worked prior to joining the Koizumi government, was brought in to support private investors in establishing de-leveraging funds, which facilitated the restructuring of debt-ridden companies. The DBJ, which was assuming a declining role, was brought fully back into its original purpose of assisting companies to grow. A new feature was that of revitalizing failing businesses, especially in the SME and rural sectors, by using the companies' intellectual property as leverage. This strategy will be assessed in light of the role of IP in regenerating the Japanese economy and business in the next section of this chapter. The recent privatization of the DBJ will be discussed in Chapter 8.

Deregulation and public corporations reform

To rid Japan of its top-heavy and public fund-draining bureaucracy, the Koizumi administration looked to the free market mechanism, which had been traditionally shunned by the LDP especially in the areas of health care, social welfare, education and other social services. Through encouraging innovation and competition by deregulating, Prime Minister Koizumi intended to revitalize the Japanese economy.

In December 2001, a plan to rationalize public corporations was announced, which resulted in 62 public corporations, or 40 per cent of the total, being largely privatized or abolished. The goal of the government was to reduce spending for public corporations by as much as one trillion yen, which amounted to roughly a 20 per cent cutback.[4]

Fiscal reform and global capital markets

In line with BOJ thinking, the issuance of government bonds was no greater than 30 trillion yen eight months into the Koizumi government. Spending was prioritized for such areas as the promotion of science, technology and education, the revitalization of the metropolitan areas and the environment, and measures for the ageing society. Public works expenditure was reduced by more than 10 per cent and projects were prioritized. Reductions were made from overseas development agencies to medical service compensation for hospitals and doctors. Private finance initiatives (PFIs) were introduced and government expenditure was kept in check. The aim of all these fiscal reforms was to achieve surplus in both central and local governments by 2010, coupled with the decline in the ratio of government debts to GDP.

These fiscal reforms, initiated and implemented within the first year of the Koizumi administration, had the desired effect. The BOJ was able to lift the blanket guarantee of the deposit in 2004 as the economy began to bottom out. The protection for current account deposits with zero interest rates has continued as a precautionary measure. By 2006, the Japanese economy and financial system as a whole having recovered, the BOJ had ceased the quantitative easing policy, which was a policy that kept the inter-bank money market from malfunctioning. The majority of banks had also recovered their capital and, despite central and local government reducing quite severely fiscal expenditure, even the small and medium-sized banks were recovering. Even the need for the comprehensive safety net was being felt less acutely.

During the Koizumi administration, the BOJ was led by Governor Fukui Toshihiko, who proved to very capable and had the confidence of central banks around the world. It was under his stewardship that, in March 2006, the BOJ ended quantitative easing and, four months after that, lifted the overnight call rate to 0.25 per cent followed by slight upward movements in interest rates. Mr Fukui noted that globalization has led to an integration of real economies throughout the world and in parallel fashion the cross-border flow of funds is also integrating the world's money and capital markets. In this case of the single world economy coming into being, Mr Fukui noted that it is insufficient for money and capital markets to operate as credit intermediaries within the confines of their countries' borders as markets should function to move funds and capital efficiently across borders. He stressed that the real economy and the financial sector are integrally linked and that the decisions of traders can present unplanned-for risks and the potential shock from such risks must be understood thoroughly before action is undertaken. Such thinking by Mr Fukui is a departure from past thinking at the BOJ and in other Japanese financial institutions, in that Japan is viewed as an integral part of the world capital markets and the process of globalization and the traditional crisis risk management that was practised by the Japanese no longer suits current economic realities.

Mr Fukui made it clear that BOJ monetary policy will be forward-looking. Although the Consumer Price Index (CPI) increase rate has been on the low side, he noted that there was no reason for it to remain so. He noted that, as the economic structure of the world is changing, Japan is also changing its economic structure through governmental reform, including deregulation. Rather than sticking to the rigid policies of the past, which has been the traditional attitude in Japan, Mr Fukui committed himself to reviewing understanding of medium- to long-term price stability while keeping an eye on both performance and future developments.[5] Such a sea change at the BOJ underscores the seriousness and efficiency with which the Koizumi administrative reforms were being carried out.

In line with the push for deregulation, the Tokyo Stock Exchange (TSE) – the leading stock exchange in Japan and known for being conservative – had their 'Big Bang' in 2001 and appointed a President, Mr Tsuchiya. The TSE, which had also fallen behind modern banking by not developing information technology (IT), brought in IT specialists from the USA to modernize their entire information systems in order to be in line with Western banking systems. The development of IT has been critical to globalization and accurate disclosure as well as to transparency and, without it, the TSE was stuck in a time warp of 'Japan Incorporated', when corporate Japan was able to profit and operate with as little reference as possible to the outside world, carrying out obligatory practices that were considered insider dealing by the rest of the world. The TSE has tried to move even further from archaic practices and rules that were prejudiced against the SME companies, which have been so pressured in recent times to produce innovative ideas. In Chapter 7 we shall explore structural changes at the TSE.[6]

New threats to economic stability

The BOJ, having learned a number of lessons from the years of economic stagnation and recovery during the Koizumi years, has understood that it is important to prepare in advance for possible economic stagnation. This means that the first step is for the public sector to share the understanding of the current economic conditions and forecasts for its foreseeable future. Disclosure of such knowledge to relevant authorities is essential to ensure transparency. If disclosure is not made paramount with one-off compensations, losses begin to accelerate and systemic risk can set in.

With such analytical insight and strong leadership offered by a world-class team in the Koizumi cabinet and with the cooperation and understanding of the BOJ, the latter, after the Koizumi years, could see that the excess liquidity in the globally integrated financial markets was emboldening investors to search for yields that were predominantly illiquid high-risk return assets, such as risky housing markets. Therefore, Japan largely foresaw the probability of the current credit crunch and has not suffered the severe consequences occurring in the USA, the UK or Germany. Having suffered a prolonged and nearly catastrophic downturn, the BOJ and many wise observers watched in trepidation property prices spiralling in the USA, the UK, Australia and Spain, the poor state of hedge funds and private equity, increasing investments in commodities or contingent liabilities and the expansion of reinsurance companies.

Although new forms of risk management[7] have been developed, the burst bubble that Japan experienced and the circumstances of the current credit crunch are outside the experience of normal risk management. The Koizumi government laid the foundations for structural reform that allowed subsequent governments, ministers, financial institutions and the BOJ to be able to see the future problems. The globalization and deregulation that the Koizumi administration inspired resulted in genuine global mechanisms being put in place, which means that warnings of impending global economic instability can be picked up much more quickly, aided by the rapid exchange of information through modern IT development. However, as the boundaries between financial institutions and funds become vague and money rapidly crosses borders, it is essential that Japan develops even more rigorous methods of disclosure and transparency.

Standardized laws, such as the new IP highway, which is being developed to protect intellectual property rights (IPR), are the way forward to deal with much-needed international cooperation among financial institutions. This will be dealt with below and in Chapter 4. There are moves in this direction, with Japan dropping its objections to the International Accounting Standards Board (IASB) and the Accounting Standards Board of Japan (ASBJ) working towards a time plan to implement new standardization, even being in the forefront of such change ahead of the USA, which appears to continue to cling to the US GAAP (generally accepted accounting principle) (see Chapter 4). As with the patent prosecution highway (PPH) being developed between Japan, the USA and the UK, a similar device needs to be initiated and implemented that establishes a cross-border safety net – perhaps a fiscal protection highway that extends beyond international bankruptcy law. Japan's banks are among the largest in the world and, if a Japanese bank fails in a smaller country or less developed country, where the bank's assets may be larger than the GDP of the entire country, the local financial authority would be incapable of dealing with such losses.

Japan and the Asian economies

The financial crisis of 1997 showed the vulnerability of many Asian countries, despite this region having the highest growth in the world at present. Japan still remains the second largest economy and, despite China having entered the World Trade Organization (WTO), holding large foreign and domestic reserves and having one of world's highest growth rates, Japan has more experience and stronger fundamentals than China. Japan's trading relations and economic cooperation with China date back thousands of years and it was Japan, through the Mitsui *zaibatsu* (a large traditional, family-owned company), that sold China coal during the 1600s as the Japanese nobles, becoming more dependent on the Mitsui banking system for financing, sold the national coalmines to Mitsui. When spindles were being developed in England to further the industrial development of textiles, Mitsui was again the major trading agent to sell the spindles to China and any other advanced textile equipment. Japan – no longer hampered by its negative role during the Second World War as aggressor through its 'co-prosperity' scheme and constrained from being a military might that would have its Asian neighbours doubt its peaceful intentions – has had for some time the chance to be the 'honest broker' in the region and take a financial lead and technology lead in sharing its advancements in these areas. The cooperation dealing with IP infringement in China and the Korean IP highway are just two examples of how Japan is accomplishing both leadership and peaceful roles in working towards stopping large-scale infringement of IPR taking place in the region.[8]

Dr Takenaka has suggested a number of roles that Japan could play in advancing the Asian economies. One is increasing foreign direct investment (FDI), which promotes growth through transferring both capital and technologies. The greater the structural adjustment and improvement of the economy in Japan, the more FDI it can invest in Asia. Japan has, for many years, invested heavily in Taiwan – a former colony – and is now doing so in China.

Japan is also prepared to promote bilateral, multilateral investment relationships and trade liberalization with Asian partners and through organizations such as the WTO. Japan has been involved in forging trade agreements with its neighbours since the late 1990s. Japan's first ever bilateral trade agreement was signed with Singapore in January 2002 as the Japan–Singapore Economic Agreement for a New Age Partnership.

Following that, Japan entered into Free Trade Agreement (FTA) talks with South Korea, while China and Japan were in discussions concerning a Japan-suggested comprehensive partnership with ASEAN (Association of South East Asian Nations) countries.

Other Asian economies also require structural reform and Japan hopes, through its own restructuring, to provide a model for the region, especially in the area of privatization.

East Asian economies in particular have always relied on government and public spending to support their research drives and give support to research and development (R&D) and to the domination of internal markets by large companies, and on bailing out banks with severe fiscal problems. This tendency is changing slowly with South Korea continuing to allow foreign investment to save Korean banks after the financial crisis of 1997. Now that Japan has had to implement structural reform that allows for genuine foreign investment because of the severity of the Japanese downturn and the need to globalize, it has been moving forward to produce models as discussed above, which could be used by other Asian countries that were overdependent on government protection and spending.[9]

Prognosis of the Koizumi years

The administration of Prime Minister Koizumi Junichiro ended in September 2006, but his reforms and his cabinet live on. To some Western observers and journalists it may appear that Mr Koizumi had done very little or was not strongly reformist enough, but in Japan the ship not only turns around slowly but it does so without making too many waves. The Japanese context is a subtle one and a few words, as well as silences, mean a lot, but most of all action shows the way. Like Winston Churchill, such a strongly charismatic and determined figure as Koizumi Junichiro, who would unsettle all the established politicians and with his team push through much-needed structural reforms, could only do his work when the country or economy was in the throes of monumental disaster. It is only in times of dire necessity that the bland rhetoric of politicians is swept aside and those talented and courageous enough are allowed to take the helm of the nation and guide it steadfastly through the choppiest of waters.

In speaking at random to Japanese people, the one thread of views about Mr Koizumi seems to be that he had to be believed because he was honest. What was this honesty and how did the populace assess it as so? The Japanese electorate are quite cynical about politicians, but one who was willing to speak directly to them in plain language and deliver without a hidden agenda appealed to the Japanese voters. Although it was former Prime Minister Hashimoto who first drew up sweeping administrative reforms, he did not have the ability to push them through and convince the population. On the contrary, all the author of this book remembers of Mr Hashimoto's years were the intense dislike and suspicion that he engendered, especially among Japanese women, whom he was antagonizing with his ill-timed increase in consumption tax, which hit household budgets and Japanese women in particular. It was amazing to see normally retiring and polite Japanese housewives being involved in noisy protests and proclaiming vociferously their disapproval of Prime Minister Hashimoto. Prime Minister Koizumi may have wished to implement many of Prime Minister Hashimoto's reforms, but he reassured a fearful and distressed electorate that Japan's disastrous economic state was only temporary and that, with structural reform and economic growth, times of prosperity – so comforting to the Japanese people after the Second World War – would return. He shielded the populace from Western sniggering that Japan, once so much in the lead, was down on its knees through slogans such as 'No economic growth without structural reform' and, most of all, he involved the populace and made them feel part of the process.

No visitor could fail to see the involvement of the population in IP days, which included all ages of people and both genders in encouraging all of them to innovate and engage in IP activities. It may have seemed odd to Westerners to see children and the population in general celebrating national IP days, but it gave Japanese people pride and a tangible activity to be involved in through which they could help to rebuild Japan's prosperity. Mr Koizumi had the talent for using every newly created device or institution in a positive manner. Those who served on the new CEFP were carefully handpicked for their talent, expertise and willingness to support the reforms as mentioned above. The key to success here was the warm and genuine support the then Prime Minister Koizumi extended to his handpicked colleagues, who were often under severe attack from those vested interests who had so much to lose from the structural reforms, while ensuring that the Japanese electorate knew they had so much to gain.

There are many successful reforms made by the Koizumi administration that are in operation to this day and there is also some unfinished business. In relation to public sector reform, Mr Koizumi successfully sidestepped the traditional bureaucratic decision-making process, which included writing a draft and consulting with the *zoku-gin* (groups affiliated with vested interests), and with particular ministers who are groups of lawmakers attached to the LDP, then followed by party approval. Using such a long-winded procedure with so many bureaucratic obstacles would have stopped public sector reform dead in its tracks. Mr Koizumi sidestepped these blockages by appealing directly to the CEFP (the Council explained above). The policies that the Koizumi administration were able to work through the CEFP gradually became more important and wider, beginning with the disposal of NPLs, followed by the establishment of Special Zones for Structural Reform, reform of the social security system, and the so-called 'trinity reforms', which involved the administrative and financial systems of central and local governments and the highly essential but contentious and traditionally resisted privatization of the postal services.

The testament to the success of bypassing the traditional decision-making routes and making decisions through the CEFP was that, despite the bureaucrats desperately trying to block the reforms to protect their vested interests, as did other special interest legislators, the remaining policies were pushed through unchanged. Proof of this was shown, for example, in the reduction in public works spending of roughly two million yen, which was achieved by fiscal year 2006.

The Koizumi administration also had the vision to realize that there is no long-term gain without short-term pain, which was certainly the case in the disposal of NPLs, which initially caused negative growth. Growth did recover to 3.2 per cent in fiscal year 2005 from 2 per cent in 2003 and 2004. Growth was initially led by exports as domestic demand and consumer demand grew in tandem. It was not just the policies of deregulation that encouraged such growth, but the confidence Mr Koizumi lent to people's perception of their well-being through involving them in the decision-making process, the growth of new businesses and new business models. This could be seen in the technical licensing organization (TLO) schemes to create new businesses, courses on how to become an entrepreneur and the DBJ's programmes, using IP as collateral to revitalize failing businesses, especially in the countryside. The deregulation did give increased confidence to foreign investors as such investment increased during the Koizumi administration. In 2002 the amount of NPLs reached 42 trillion yen with the ratio of NPLs at major banks standing at 8.4 per cent. By March 2006 these figures had fallen to 15 trillion yen and 1.8 per cent respectively. The capital adequacy ratios of banks and, with higher risk tolerance, the financial intermediary functions of the banks, have all been restored to respectable levels.

The BOJ's *tankan* (investigation or exploratory) survey of business sentiment found that the majority of both large-scale and SME manufacturing enterprises had a favourable experience of business conditions from mid-2003 and 2004 onwards respectively. In terms of corporate performance, both total ordinary profits and the average ratio of ordinary profits to sales of all enterprises increased for four straight years from 2002 to 2005. In fact these figures exceeded those during the height of the economic bubble in the 1980s. Increased confidence in the Japanese economy allowed for increased sales along with lowered labour costs, which underpinned this recovery. Labour costs were largely reduced by increasing the number of lower-paid temporary and part-time workers, who amounted to one-third of all those in employment in 2005. Temporary and part-time unemployment is native to the Japanese economy as, in times of boom, the full-time employment rates increase with a pool of temporary/part-time workers while, in times of bust, the full-time employment rates ebb. The only difference in the most recent surge in the temporary workers syndrome is that they are also to be found in financial services, real estate and communications industries.

What is perceived as a worrying trend by many is the growing disparity in incomes in Japanese society. This, however, is most likely due to an increase in the numbers of temporary/part-time workers and of the elderly who draw on national resources while generating little income, which skews the figures. As lifetime employment and an assured place in a large company becomes a practice of the past, young people under 25 years old often find themselves as part of the temporary workforce. Many of these young people become 'freeters', flitting from one temporary job to the next, or part of the NEET population who are not in education, employment or training.

An area that Mr Koizumi did not tackle, and perhaps wisely, was raising the consumption tax, which had caused Mr Hashimoto so much antagonism that his time in office is largely remembered for the massive protests and antagonism surrounding this issue. This totally overshadowed all the good work he had done in laying the foundations of structural reform. Former Prime Minister Koizumi also steered clear of further cuts in public expenditure, which would have made the public mistrust him as they would have perceived him as lowering their standards of living. Mr Koizumi was trusted because he did not renege on the promises he had made and did not make overambitious promises that he could not deliver. For example, he kept his pledge at the time of his inauguration to reduce the issuance of government bonds to less than 30 trillion yen, which he accomplished in 2006 before leaving office.[10]

In the next chapter we assess the second pillar of the Koizumi administration's success, which was the promotion of IP. Without innovation and healing the rifts between university inventors and business, employers and employee inventors, Japan was doomed to stagnation and falling behind in global competitiveness. The vigour with which Mr Koizumi and his team injected life into IPR, patenting and innovation, in such a short space of time, introducing new legislation to make IP flourish and bringing together all the disparate institutions to accomplish this, was quite remarkable.

2 Japan as an IP nation

Japan is inventing its way out of an economic inertia that has existed for at least a decade. It is making some of the most radical changes in history to its assessment of valuing intangible assets and changing its attitudes to litigation. The speed of change in the IP field is occurring at a furious pace and in some cases surpassing that in Western countries. The push of the Koizumi administration for Japan to become an IP nation and the vigorous nature of IP promotion were linked inextricably to economic structural reform, which was part of the need to be globally competitive once again by turning around the catastrophic economic situation.

Traditional Japanese attitudes in relation to litigation

Historically, the relationship of the Japanese to legal matters has been an ambivalent one; born out of necessity but with a sense of shame, litigation was prohibited between vassals and overlords. Japan has had to overcome this societal constraint to adopt Western patent law, to enable it to industrialize and become a global force.

It has always been the case that cyclical periods of economic crisis increased patent activity, which was then followed by prosperity; this cycle has repeated itself since the sixteenth century, when Japan first began to industrialize, with the Mitsui *zaibatsu*, as mentioned in Chapter 1, taking the lead through its incipient role as bankers to the nobles and as major traders with China and beyond.

In the sixteenth century the Japanese became the world's leading manufacturers of firearms in the world; they had learned such manufacturing techniques from the Portuguese. However, in the repressive Edo Shogunate, which lasted 250 years, the Japanese fell behind the West in technological development. In 1854, Japan emerged from its isolation and looked to patenting to invent its way out of economic stagnation and technological underdevelopment. The first patent ordinance was passed on 18 April 1885, but as it did not recognize the rights of foreigners a new Patent Law was introduced in 1899 that did so, and thereafter Japan joined the Paris Convention. After the Second World War, Japan, again in crisis, invented its way into a prosperity admired and envied by Western countries, with such notable inventors as Matsushita Konosuke, the founder of the Matsushita group, who set up his company based on the proprietary rights to a new electronic socket. In the development of his global electronics business, he acquired over 100 patents.

However, after the spectacular success that the Japanese experienced during the 1960s, when they became lauded for their inventiveness, total quality management procedures based on models proposed by Deming and general business success, fortunes declined, bringing on economic stagnation. Invention ground to a halt, with universities giving little incentive to encourage their staff to patent and license their inventions. The relationship between the university inventors and companies was poor and invention internal to companies was not properly rewarded. Entrepreneurship was not encouraged, and, coupled with the cultural idea that 'the nail that sticks up should be hammered down', this meant that some of the most inventive Japanese were lured by the rewards offered by America. The patent system had not changed since 1960 and was becoming hopelessly out of date in a world where intangible assets were beginning to comprise 70 per cent of most major companies' assets. The wake-up call came, as mentioned in Chapter 1, during the Hashimoto administration, when the reality of the world's second largest economy becoming globally uncompetitive forced the Japanese government to act.

However, as mentioned, it took the less traditional methods of governance undertaken by Prime Minister Koizumi and his cabinet to turn around Japan's fortunes and he was as thorough and innovative in his methods for the promotion of IP as he was in economic structural reform. What Prime Minister Koizumi and Arai Hisamitsu, former Commissioner of the Japan Patent Office (JPO) and head of IP strategy in the Koizumi cabinet, did to harness all potential patents and promote IP was the following, which will be discussed in detail below.

They sought to re-involve universities, where many of the patentable inventions were not brought to fruition and were stagnating, and they moved from an improvement-based innovation to 'blue-sky' research, which was based on totally new ideas and innovative products and services. This was all linked to legislative reform encouraging university–business partnerships and judicial reform and making the general population take an active part in the national IP drive through increased awareness and simplified procedures. The Koizumi government and the judiciary encouraged both advanced technology and an active licensing market by rewarding inventors and protecting IP from infringers, especially in the global marketplace. They also sought, for example with economic policies such as international accounting standards, to harmonize IP systems and procedures in line with the globalization of business. The Koizumi administration with Mr Arai heading the IP drive had the intention of improving on Japan's ownership of 24 per cent of the world's patent rights, ranking it second in the world.

TLO laws, privatization of universities and new IP divisions

The TLO law, or 'Promoting University–Industry Technology Transfer', has ushered in a new relationship between inventors, universities and industry. Japan initially followed the strategies of the USA and then adapted these TLO policies to the Japanese case. As Terry Young, former President of the Association of University Technology Managers (AUTM) and manager of technology transfer at Texas A&M University, noted, technology transfer is needed to reward, retain and recruit faculty members. TLOs are good vehicles for creating closer ties to industry. To understand the process of commercialization, which allows the assessment of the value of IP, it is important to encourage a better and closer relationship between universities and industry.

In the USA, TLOs are serving as engines for economic development by spinning out new companies and creating new employment opportunities. Finally, TLOs manage a process of commercializing and transferring research results for public good and benefit.[1] Within Japan a Bayh Dole-like Act of 1980 was legislated with input from leading academics such as Professor Nishizawa Akio, Deputy Director at the New Hatchery Centre at Tohoku University in Sendai, who had great experience of the implementation of the Bayh Dole Act in the USA. He was instrumental in shaping the Japanese legislation that allowed universities to partially own the rights to governmentally funded research and then license it to private companies who would then commercialize it.

As of 2003, Japan had adapted the TLO idea to 33 mainly university centres, whereby TLOs that are approved can use national university properties without any cost. (The centres were privatized in April 2004.) The role of TLOs has expanded further from solely tech-transfer functions to centres that assist university start-ups. Professor Nishizawa points to a development unique to Japan – that of intra-university IP divisions. The latter will exist solely to give advice and support to those in the university who wish to bring their inventions to fruition. The Ministry of

Education, Sport, Science and Technology (MEXT) has awarded such IP divisions to 34 Japanese universities.

Professor Nishizawa points to further structural changes that need to be implemented in the Japanese economy, which are all inextricably linked to IP. These changes include moving from a follow-through to a breakthrough system, from centralized to decentralized, and from government (bureaucracy)-led to market-oriented, changing from big business with scale of economy to entrepreneurial ventures with scope of economy and from capital labour intensive to knowledge intensive. The success of the Japanese TLOs may be seen in the rise in the numbers of patent applications filed, from 273 in fiscal year 1999 to 1,335 in fiscal year 2002, with gross licence income respectively increasing from 20,784 to 410,191 yen.[2]

Making use of unrealized inventions

The first attempt at dealing with unrealized inventions has been by Dr Ishimaru Kimio, Director of the National Institute of Advanced Industrial Science and Technology (AIST). AIST was instituted on 1 April 2001 and is a new research organization that comprises 15 research institutes that were formerly under the Agency of Industrial Science and Technology in the Ministry of International Trade and Industry and the Weights and Measures Training Institute. The new AIST is Japan's largest public research organization, with many research facilities and around 6,000 employees in total.

The portfolio in 2003, according to Dr Ishimaru, consisted of 10,000 research projects in various states of completion from all affiliated institutes. Since 2001, when the IP drive began under the Koizumi government, 150 licensing agreements have been made and are being concluded at a rate of 30 agreements a year, increasing by ten a year. Many of the inventions are fundamental ones – for example, a core LCD patent belonging to AIST, which is a leaner, less bureaucratic institution in line with overall structural reforms, designed to maximize the advantages of an independent administrative body and to ensure the autonomous functioning of the organization.[3]

Valuing intellectual property

The valuing of IP became and continues to be increasingly an issue of greater concern and importance. Kato Taisuke, General Manager of Toshiba IP Division, Corporate Headquarters in Tokyo, notes how Toshiba understands the importance of placing a value on IP. In developed economies, the migration from manufacturing to services is paralleled by a shift in asset evaluation from physical assets to intangible assets. A well-known example of this, according to Kato, is the estimate that two-thirds of the market capital of listed companies in the USA can be accounted for by intangible assets, including IP.

While there is increasing discussion on how best to value IP, a unified methodology has yet to emerge. The market value method has its supporters, as it tries to consider not only present royalty streams but also possible future royalty income. However, there remain difficulties in evaluating certain IP assets, particularly future potential. Toshiba is now looking at promotion of a system of relative evaluation that measures their strength in IP against that of their competitors. The consideration here is quantity versus quality. Quantity can easily be determined, while quality is more problematic, but possible to some extent.

Toshiba is a Japanese company that has integrated successful IP valuation into the three-tier incentive system that they use to encourage and reward innovation among their researchers and engineers. The first tier is transfer remuneration, under which an inventor can receive as much as 15,000 yen for transferring an idea to Toshiba. Business remuneration is paid if and when that invention is used in a product, and licensing remuneration is paid from any licensing income Toshiba might receive for IP. The other two incentives depend on the market and the extent to which the IP is utilized.

Every year, the company arrives at a value for productive IP by calculating how much it contributed to actual sales and earned in royalty income. This gives them the basis for open-ended business and licensing remuneration incentives.[4]

Toshiba also practises an essential feature of Japanese IP strategy encouraged during the Koizumi and Arai years, which ensures that their IP assets enjoy a freedom to conduct business through 'open licensing policies'. The latter refer to the cross-licensing of technologies with balance of payments compensation for any shortfall in the quality of a technology. Toshiba is again a good example of IP trading use, which they use to form close links with both their domestic and foreign counterparts and which promotes globalization. For example, sharing patents with IBM led to joint venture agreements and other business collaborations.

Patent pools

In the past and in the years of stagnation, Japan was used to the idea of in-licensing – bringing in technologies from other countries to innovate.

The emphasis during the Koizumi years was to improve on Japanese innovations and technical expertise, especially in the area of electronics, which has been overtaking the West, meaning that Western companies have begun to in-license new Japanese technology. This has seen income from fees and royalties flowing into Japanese companies, rather than the other way around, which serves to provide companies with long-term revenue that they can build to develop their own advanced technologies even further.

The cost of developing new product ideas that are globally competitive and innovative is very high, so patent pools have been on the increase in Japan. Patent pools serve to ensure that more patents come to fruition as the likelihood of litigation and other attempts at blocking the commercialization of the innovation is reduced. More resources can be pooled together to create a new product with all in the patent pool receiving proportionately larger shares from fees and royalties.[5]

Proactive prosecution of infringers

Japanese companies began a process during the Koizumi years to license their patents globally and to internal markets. This was done through change to management behaviour and structure. Licensing staff were required to generate revenue from patents that matched or exceeded the cost of administering the patents. Staff were recruited who could both negotiate with foreign companies and draft licensing agreements. Some Japanese companies employed foreign consultants to find appropriate third parties to license to. The JPO began to provide guidelines to assist Japanese companies in setting higher royalty rates as there was no firm policy on this in the past.

A proactive attitude to patent infringers was encouraged by the Koizumi administration and the JPO. Traditionally, the reluctance to enter into litigation stopped many companies from pursuing infringers in the courts. Also, in the past, when Japan was heavily in-licensing, it was most often Japanese companies that were accused of copying and infringing, but with greater innovative success and higher patenting among Japanese companies it was the latter who had the vested interest in pursuing infringers. As the success of Japan's economic recovery depends on again becoming globally competitive, any infringement, especially in the highly lucrative electronics area, is a potential threat to recovery.

Mr Koizumi took a particularly hardline approach against China, making few concessions, which could be seen as China being perceived as a serious global competitor.

Global harmonization

As well as being a central feature of economic structural reform, globalization has also been an essential part of Japanese patent strategy, assisting Japanese companies to compete on a global scale. As mentioned above, Japan joined the Paris Convention in 1899, the purpose of which was to globally harmonize patent systems and procedures. Subsequent international treaties, such as the Trilateral Patent Offices (US, European and Japanese) Kyoto Action Plan in November 1997, recognized a 'Worldwide System for the Grant of Patents'. There are parallels with Japan joining more fully the IASB as described in Chapter 1.

By the beginning of the Koizumi government, Japanese companies became increasingly active in filing foreign applications, especially in the USA. In 2001, Japanese companies accounted for seven out of the top ten firms being granted US patents, with NEC leading with 1,953 patents. As in other countries it is mainly the large companies that are filing, as Japanese SMEs do not have the resources to do so. As Japan became more inventive it became the target of infringement, so global harmonization serving to increase the predictability of application results also provides protection for Japanese patents in foreign countries.

Similarly to encouraging economic ties with their Asian neighbours so they can help control trade to their advantage, the Japanese are doing the same with patenting in Asia. The Japanese created the ASEAN Patent and Trademark Office and have been heavily involved in the education of Asian developing countries in IP and technology. The JPO and Japanese industry have been sending delegations of experts to provide training to Asian IP professionals and even extend this help to financial support. These practices serve to facilitate Japan's global competitiveness in allowing it to gain protection for its innovations and a marketplace for its goods.[7]

Judicial reform

Japan's commitment to invention is profound. Prime Minister Koizumi launched the national strategy for invention and IP in a policy speech to the Diet in early 2002, resulting in March of that year in the formation of the Strategic Council on Intellectual Property. On 17 April 2003, a Day of Invention occurred to galvanize the nation into consensus-based action for the promotion of invention and IP. Organizations such as the Japanese Patent Information Organization (JPIO) and the Japanese Institute for Invention and Innovation (JIII) were set up to provide advice and encourage the populace to understand all aspects of IP. Along with all the sweeping reforms of Patent Law in general[7] come other historic changes to the Patent Attorneys Law, none having occurred since the beginning of the Meiji Era, and the new introduction of Patent Courts in 2005.

Shimosaka Sumiko, who was then President of the Japan Patent Attorneys Association (JPAA), outlined a number of key areas for JPAA to concentrate on. These included the problems of counterfeiting and infringement of IP in Asia, and participating more in international conferences and working together with more international IP organizations. Paramount has been the training of patent lawyers to have the expertise to cope with the new complex reforms. Progress on this has been rapid, as will be outlined in Chapter 4. The increase in patent attorneys (*benrishi*) obtaining the new expertise was already marked, with 533 *benrishi* having passed an examination that complies with a recent law allowing patent attorneys to jointly and equally represent clients with attorneys at law (*bengoshi*). The fact that *benrishi* were now able to represent their clients equally changed the whole process of IP litigation. At a symposium in 2004, Shimosaka Sumiko noted that *benrishi* were on course to assume an important role in creating, protecting and utilizing IP.[8]

In January/February 2004, the Strategic Council on Intellectual Property and the Office for Promotion of Justice Systems Reform advisory panel to Prime Minister Koizumi decided that an independent high court should be created by April 2005. This decision followed many months of acrimonious debate, with some arguing for a new independent high court specializing in IP infringement cases that would make the litigation process easier for businesses and become a ninth high court (Japan has high courts for eight major jurisdictions). Others from a more bureaucratic perspective believed that litigation resulting from IP disputes could be accommodated by reinforcing the existing special division at the Tokyo High Court. A compromise solution was finally agreed under the tentatively named 'Intellectual Property High Court', which is currently operating within the Tokyo High Court but with a high degree of independence. This new high court deals with appeals of district court rulings over rights infringement lawsuits and lawsuits filed by those who are dissatisfied with the JPO's decisions on their applications for patent rights.

The decision was welcomed by the JPAA, which had lobbied for an independent high court for intellectual property infringement lawsuits. The JPAA sees the independence of personnel management and the mobilization of judges and examiners who are experts on matters dealing with intellectual property as a priority. The Intellectual Property High Court was seen as even more necessary because already in 2001, of some

440,000 applications for patent rights registration filed with the JPO, at least 20,000 complaints were filed by applicants against its decisions of refusal. With numbers of applicants increasing, acrimonious complaints were also growing in number, so restructuring through fast-tracking and other methods discussed in Chapter 4 served to ease this problem.

Japan as the world's most innovative nation

With Japan mobilized to become an IP nation, in all the ways mentioned above, by the middle of 2007[9] Japan was ranked as the world's most innovative nation according to a study conducted by the Economist Intelligence Unit. Innovation was defined as 'the application of knowledge in a novel way primarily for economic benefit'. The top four innovators from among the 82 economies observed from 2002 to 2006 were Japan, Switzerland, the USA and Sweden. The most appropriate measure of innovation was the number of patents generated by a country per million people. Japan's ratio of patents per million people is 3.5 per cent higher than the USA's – mainly because the population of Japan is only 42 per cent of that of the US – and is the highest such ratio in the world. Japan was number one in innovation despite having a poorer telecommunications infrastructure and fewer environmental factors conducive to innovation. The latter refers to, for example, oil-rich countries in the Middle East, which have enormous capital reserves from oil and gas wealth but barely rank in relation to innovative practices globally. Japan has always been natural resource poor with virtually no mineral wealth other than bauxite or kaolin. Perhaps Japan follows the maxim 'necessity is the mother of invention', for without Japanese drive and ingenuity it could never have become the second largest economy in the world. The level of education of the Japanese population and numbers of researchers in relation to the population are very high, coupled with the amount of investment in R&D, which is proportionately higher than in the USA.

The study has predicted that, for 2007–11, the same ranking will be maintained (and this has been confirmed in results from 2008, in which Japan continues to be the top producer of patents), except that China will become in absolute terms the second largest investor in R&D after the USA. China is already leading in a number of innovative products such as medical devices. Japan has to look over its shoulder constantly in the case of China, but if Japan's success continues, if it does not slide back into inertia, which almost happened during the administration of Abe Shinzo following that of Mr Koizumi, and if the current Prime Minister, Mr Aso Taro, and his successor continue to be a pair of safe hands, carrying on reforms, China may not overtake Japan.

The study noted however that, in terms of perception, the majority of the 485 senior global executives taking the Economist Intelligence Unit survey cited the USA as the best place for innovation and cast doubt on Japan's innovative potential. Only 2 per cent of respondents saw Japan as having the best conditions, while 40 per cent and 12 per cent, respectively, viewed the USA and India as being the best places for innovation. This is not a surprising result, as Japan has always undersold itself and is not only still perceived as an inaccessible country with a very different business culture and language, but is also so indirect and modest that many Westerners fail to see its strengths and successes. The Koizumi administration succeeded in mobilizing the Japanese population to commit itself to structural reform, an unprecedented IP drive and a dramatic turnaround in the Japanese economy. However, in terms of changing opinion about its potential for innovation and business success, it has not succeeded. Yet, in discussing the new IP highways in Chapter 4 it will become clear that Japan is making a step in that direction. The new AIM-like market that the TSE is trying to initiate may be another step in that direction and this will be discussed in Chapter 7 within the context of global perception as well as reality. Before the future is assessed it is useful to look at the history to understand and give insights into future developments.

3 Historical perspectives of the economy and IP

From village to industrialized nation

In the first half of the nineteenth century, Japan was like any pre-industrial Asian country. The bulk of the populace lived in rural villages and Osaka was the financial centre with Edo as the seat of the Shogunate government. Economic policy and decision-making under the *bakuhan* system were shared by the Tokugawa government (*bakufu*) and nearly 300 domains of the *han*. The economy was operated through regulation and control at all levels of administration. It was a controlled economy that was not reliant on market forces and therefore could not create economic growth.[1]

Borrowing from Europe to industrialize

The reasons why Japan never fully developed into a free market economy with the tendency for the government to interfere with the market process, trying to control the economy in the interests of the state, can be seen in the historical economic roots of Japan. The 'laissez faire' economic principles followed by the English in the nineteenth century did not find favour with the Meiji Restoration period even though the idea of a market began to be accepted. The English idea of a free market was not even accepted before the Second World War. Rather, as in the legal sphere it was the German Historical School that found the greatest resonance with economic thought in Japan. In the late nineteenth century the German model was considered more appropriate because it could be used to justify state intervention and nationalistic policies in terms of monopoly protection and subsidies to private enterprises. The interests of the state, which became very strong during Tokugawa times, were served well by the bureaucracy,[2] which was a link to the modern-day Koizumi government, although the state and the established bureaucracy were weakened through an unheard-of involvement and mobilization of the populace and a non-established group of colleagues in a non-aligned CEFP, as mentioned in Chapter 1.

Why not the English model of industrialization?

It is instructive to examine the English form of feudalism, which gave rise to an economy that readily embraced a free market and the tenets of a modern industrialization 'laissez faire' policy. The openness in the English hierarchical structure allowed for freedom of movement up and down the social scale, which was linked to a particularly English form of 'political feudalism'. Only in England was there a genuine 'decentralization' of the state, which formed a loose structure linked externally with the division of state power between head and members resting on their power over land and people. This was different from the tightly structured, centralized nature of the 'state' in Japan, in which state power was divided according to the function, such as tax collection. In England the institution of estates both supported and limited the power of the monarchy. Political feudalism was dominated by dynastic household interests, with the role of the administrators of the clerical estate far outweighing that of the knightly nobility. In England the loose control exercised by the political state was caused mainly by conflict of interests, economically and politically, between the monarchy, nobility and clergy, which were always at one time or another fighting among themselves for control. This allowed increasing movement of the population and free economic activity that boosted growth. Farmers were allowed to own their land and a form of meritocracy allowed the talented and able to create a self-perpetuating elite who, through their innovative ideas, encouraged economic growth by product development.

The Japanese form of feudalism was not only more centralized but gave prominence to knightly nobility, or the *bushi*, who constituted the *samurai* warrior class, demanding absolute loyalty and obedience from the vassals. It was a closed system of absolute control by the *daimyo*, or feudal lords, implemented by the *bushi* with a strict hierarchical order. The social organization of the vassalage reflected the obedience expected by the father from other family members. Each group of *bushi* was linked by blood relationships and this constituted a coherent unit directed by the head, or *katoku*. The *katoku* had the right and duty to expect obedience from the members of his group when orders came from the *bakufu*, or central government. The *katoku*, for example, was responsible for collecting the taxes from his group to give to the government tax collector.

He therefore ensured that all in the village worked hard and cooperated to produce the required tax.

While serfdom was declining in England between 1200 and 1500, vassalage remained strong in Japan, with the Genji clan establishing and exercising their centralized authority and power, after their victory over the Taira clan in 1185. When the *bushi* all came under the Genji clan, a hierarchical order was established, with the leader Yoritomo Minamoto at the top. In this particular order of ranking and hierarchy, the inferior owed his superior a duty of devoted service. The lords gave the vassals some benefits in the way of rewards, but it still constituted a very paternalistic relationship. This gave rise to the *oyabun/kobun* relationship – the *oyabun* had the status of parent and the *kobun* of child. The *oyabun* looked after the *kobun* and his dependants, assisting with important life matters, while the *kobun* was always ready to offer services to the *oyabun*. This type of relationship, but between employer and employees, has continued within the context of the *kaisha* (large companies) today.

Military officials were given prominence, with Yoritomo providing the warriors (*jito*) with manorial properties (*sho*) that did not belong to them. Law in the Kamakura *bakufu* period, which preceded the Muromachi *bakufu* (1338–1573), was not comparable to modern law as it was based on emotional rather than moral factors. During the Muromachi *bakufu* the state weakened and warlords prospered.

The next major period, known as the Tokugawa Era, after Tokugawa Ieyasu who united the country, lasted from 1603 to 1868. It was a purely feudal regime. The *bakufu* was strongly centralized and the head was the most powerful *daimyo* known as the *shogun*, which roughly means 'generalissimo'. This *bakufu* was very authoritarian, practising a strict form of Confucianism. Peasants comprised about 80 per cent of the population but were virtually serfs. The government was merciless, placing heavy burdens of taxation on the peasants and demanding service. Social mobility did not exist as it was forbidden to change class. Merchants were counselled that they should never aspire to changing their rank in society.

However intelligent, talented or enterprising merchants were, they were told that their fate was sealed from birth by heaven and that they could never move beyond their class background. Meritocracy, or the ability to be upwardly mobile because of inventiveness, was rare and was positively discouraged.

As the peasants in England gained their freedom, land and property agreements were based on contract rather than the relationship imposed by the lord of the manor on the tenant. In Japan, the *daimyo* had no obligations legally and were not bound to enter into any contract with the peasant farmers, yet the latter did have legal obligations to the *daimyo*.[3]

During the Shogunate and Tokugawa or Edo period of the fourteenth and fifteenth centuries, a strict class system was retained, which would have inhibited the need for litigation as the class system was rigid with a very clear system of superiority and subordination in all social relationships. Vassalage was dominated by this principle of rigid social ranking, as were all other relationships between master and servant, parent and child, husband and wife. The classes that constituted society were the *kuge* (nobles of the imperial court), the *samurai*, the clergy (Buddhist and Shinto), the commoners and farmers, both rich and poor. Nobles were not under any bond of vassalage to the *shogun*, but were under the strict control of the *bakufu*. Commoners were divided into three categories in order of standing: farmers, artisans and merchants. The poor farmers had to live a miserable life, working from dawn to dusk in extreme frugality. The whole order was legitimized by the idea of natural law, in which class was ordained by nature and birth. Intelligence or talent were irrelevant.[4]

The modern legal system

The tradition of legal obligations was biased towards the feudal lord and therefore provided no legal foundations for a modern free market economy or for intellectual property laws. By the early nineteenth century, the Japanese government was under pressure to compete globally and was required to borrow a legal system. The French Napoleonic codes were chosen because they were less complicated than English common law and many other modernizing nations were using them as a basis for legal reform.

In the latter part of the nineteenth century, Gustav Boissonade, a professor of law from Paris, was requested to reform the entire Japanese law code along French lines. His attempt to do this was rejected by Japanese conservatives, a group similar to those politicians and bureaucrats Mr Koizumi had to circumvent, who claimed that Boissonade did not include enough of an emphasis on Japanese custom, morality and tradition. The Japanese administration then attempted to borrow from other legal codes, such as English common law, but found them too complex and value laden to implement in Japan. The choice in the end was German technocratic law, which was relatively value free. A liberal element arose from the lower *samurai* class, but was crushed violently and a turning towards Prussian-German technocratic law in terms of constitutional and administrative law followed to further the aim of the absolutist state in Japan. In February 1889, the Meiji constitution was finally drafted and accepted but was based on the Prussian constitution, which continued to allow the military an independent role, one that allowed direct dealings with the emperor. In placing the military beyond the control of civil ministers, military despotism was encouraged.

The adoption of capitalism to become competitive

Japan's motive in adopting capitalism was to equal the great powers of the world though being rich and strong. The spirit of liberalism and free competition was lacking, as well as sufficient capital for accumulation. The state was not even seen as a possible source of the social contract. Japanese capitalism prospered at the expense of the farmers and workers, who were severely exploited. Therefore, external markets became necessary, as internal markets were insufficient to absorb the increased production of manufactured goods. The old Japanese morality was retained and the educational system stressed society as a large family, in which the rights of individuals were irrelevant. Merchants were despised by the upper classes as being involved in the shameful business of making money without honour or honesty and conducting business with strangers. This very closed feudal-based attitude changed when the money extracted from farmers decreased considerably and the nobles then encouraged their daughters to marry wealthy merchants.

During the Edo period, strong pressure was placed on the populace to follow all orders with obedience and docility. It was stressed that it was contrary to loyalty and fidelity for an inferior to criticize a superior (e.g. the government). Law was used only as a means of constraint by the authorities to achieve government purposes. People only had the choice of obeying and they developed a psychological complex – *menju-fukuhai* – meaning that they obeyed their superiors outwardly, while rebelling against them inwardly. No class of professional lawyers or barristers existed; there were notaries but they had limited functions, mainly in relation to property dealings; and, in plays, there were no advocates or notaries, who often played an important part in Western drama.

Having no real legal tradition of their own and no established profession, the Japanese embraced Western law. During the Meiji Restoration period, Japan's ignorance of legal matters, or their narrow, inflexible interpretation, worked against Japan in its commercial treaties with the USA, Britain, France, Russia and the Netherlands. Because the

Japanese were ignorant of international law, they accepted unfavourable conditions.

As the Japanese economy was modernizing quickly and the lack of a modern legal system was working against Japan's interests, the Japanese government was compelled to create an instantaneous legal system despite the social status of Japan's emperor as the divine father. The state took on a sacred and mystical form (*kokutai*), linked to old customs that were devoid of any form of scientific analysis or criticism in general and whose espousal was severely punished. Litigation was not a form of law that was actively encouraged. Therefore, it is within this context that current Japanese patent law must be understood.

Institution of patent law in the twentieth century

The Japanese government worked throughout the twentieth century to institute an IP system that has the trust and support of the public, business and academia. It was not until the 1960s, however, that the patent system in Japan was further developed to suit the needs of industrialists who sought to make their companies and Japan more competitive. Foremost among these industrialists were:

- Matsushita Konosuke, the founder of the Matsushita group, who set up his company based on the proprietary rights to a new electric socket. In the development of his global electronics business, he acquired over 100 patents.
- Ibuka Masaru, one of the founders of Sony, who was trained in patent specifications and applications and who used to study the *Patent Gazette* to identify technological trends. This IP knowledge was the basis of the foundation and development of the company now known as Sony. Over his lifetime, Ibuka acquired 50 patents and 53 utility models.
- Honda Soichiro, who in 1948 established Honda and spent some time researching petrol combustion, and who developed a motorbike so superior that it won all five classes of the famous TT races on the Isle of Man. This success gave Honda and Japan international recognition and stimulated the development of Honda's motorbike and automobile group, through which he amassed 115 patents and 359 utility models.[5]

After this industrialist-led boom in patenting, IP began a decline until the Koizumi government's IP drive.

Establishment of the modern unified financial system

When the feudal system was abolished in the late nineteenth/early twentieth century, the *samurai* lost their direct position of power but still had influence, while the merchants of the Tokugawa Era changed their role with the collapse of the commercial system. Traditional patterns of trade were ended with the abolition of the guild system, the opening of the ports and the introduction of freedom of commerce, which saw the beginnings of a new brand of speculative trader. With the government ordering a forced reduction of debts, which resulted in heavy losses for the merchants, in the first years of the reforms several hundred merchant houses became bankrupt.

Okuma Shigenobu (1838–1922), who led the Ministry of Finance together with a group of dynamic, American-oriented associates, began the establishment of a unified modern financial system in Japan. A new national currency, the yen, was instituted in 1871, which ended the previous system of money-changing by merchant houses, which had previously functioned as currency exchanges (*ryogaeya*). The national mint began its operations in Osaka in the same year. The government introduced a land tax system in 1873, which would provide a stable source of tax income whereby taxes were to be paid in currency instead of rice. Farmers were now required to collect large amounts of money, which created the pool of capital to establish a banking system.

To assist the merchants whose expertise the government required to deal with trade from the West, and to encourage foreign trade, eight cities were designated in which joint stock commerce companies were established. The government placed a high priority on foreign trade, but the breakthrough for the joint stock companies came with the banks.

It was the Meiji government, in its quest to create a modern banking system, that promoted the establishment of 'exchange companies' (*kawase kaisha*), in the form of joint stock enterprises, to act as banks. These companies were not modern stock corporations in the modern sense, but there were some similarities. They were in part capitalized with government money and their participants or 'shareholders' were entitled to a fixed dividend, while at the same time participating in profits. The government guaranteed interest on capital and certificates were issued but could only be transferred with the company's consent. The president (*shacho*) was not elected but was the holder of the majority of the certificates after being appointed by the Ministry of Finance. Despite their structure as joint stock companies, the participants bore an unlimited liability. This banking experiment by the Meiji government ultimately failed because the individual merchant houses were not allowed to operate independently and pursue profit unfettered by government interference.

Banking system based on the US model

It was not until the government of Ito Hirobumi (1841–1909) that a new system of national banks was introduced based on the US model. The original National Banking Decree of 1872 was also unsuccessful because of merchants who were reluctant to be shareholders and too much government interference. The Decree was amended in 1876, stipulating that banks had to be organized as joint stock companies with a minimum of five shareholders. Shares held a face value of 100 yen and could be acquired by everyone as well as freely transferred with the permission of the directors. Each share provided for the same voting right and the director shareholders were elected by the shareholders' assembly. There was a limited liability established in the National Banking Decree with these national banks. With greater freedom for enterprise, these banks in turn gave rise to enterprise in other sectors of the economy.

By 1880 there were more than 150 national banks in operation, mainly founded not by merchants but by *samurai*. The *samurai* became the driving force for the establishment of new banks, as it was their feudal stipends after 1876 that were compulsorily converted into government bonds, which were then invested in banks as founding capital. Banks were now allowed to issue their own inconvertible bank notes and they began to be profitable. In addition to the national banks, a number of private banks were founded during the 1880s, such as the first private bank, Mitsui, which was a large city bank and a natural progression from the old Mitsui trading company *zaibatsu*. By the turn of the century about 1,800 private banks were in operation, mainly financed by local landowners and businessmen. They served as a crucial link to channel local savings into national projects. It was during this time that the government began to understand the importance of IP as a means of building commerce and foreign trade, in addition to protecting Japanese IPR.

The development of corporate law

The government sought to develop the company system and, although there was uncertainty concerning liability in terms of business failure, the Old Commercial Code, which was instituted in 1893, served to clarify matters by creating clear legal distinctions between companies. The Commercial Code Enforcement Ordinance Act, for example, stipulated that every company already incorporated at the time had to register within six months of the enforcement of the Old Commercial Code. The registration had to be done according to the appropriate type of company provided for in the code. What emerged was a regularizing of companies, as prior to 1893 many private undertakings were counted as commercial companies but did not qualify under the new prescriptions for registration.

Artisans and small family-based companies still constituted the bulk of private Japanese companies, with the majority having no more than five workers. The larger merchant houses such as Mitsui, for example, continued to conduct business on a partnership basis, with members of the widespread family enterprises acting as partners. They all increasingly used new legal forms provided for in the code of limited partnership companies (*goshi kaisha*) and, to a lesser extent, the general partnership companies (*gomei kaisha*).

Stock companies in the vanguard of modernization

In parallel to the Industrial Revolution that took place in England during the nineteenth century, an increasing number of successful stock corporations besides banks were founded in the areas of cotton spinning and railways and had, on average, several hundred shareholders. The stock corporation developed into the most important form of enterprise in Meiji Japan and, between 1895 and 1910, the capital of the stock corporations, on average, accounted for nearly 90 per cent of paid-in capital. The acceptance and success of the stock corporations were largely due to two phenomena. One, already mentioned, was the involvement of the *samurai*, who invested their pensions in nascent banks. The other was that merchants were considered to be the lowest of the four social classes in Tokugawa times, while employment in a modern industrial stock corporation was seen as honourable, responsible and at the same time serving the needs of the nation in building a modern economy; in other words, a worthy nationalistic goal. Much like the Koizumi government, the Meiji government popularized the new form of enterprise in traditional terms, which the Japanese people could relate to and feel part of. The use of the word *kabu* for the English word 'share' had its roots in the traditional Tokugawa partnerships, where participation in a guild was known as *kabu nakama*.

Stock exchanges influenced by London

The Japanese government issued bonds on a large scale between 1875 and 1877 and it required a market for these bonds. The majority of the bonds were given to the *samurai* as compensation for their stipends and these resources had to be mobilized. It was in 1878 that the first stock exchanges were opened in Tokyo and Osaka. The exchanges were organized as joint stock companies. Their numbers grew quickly so that, in 1898, there were roughly 46 exchanges in operation.

The development of the stock exchanges, as with the banks and other corporations, is subject to much debate. As with the legal system, before the stock exchanges were formed, foreign exchanges were studied to see which would be the best model for Japan. In the case of trading in shares, the rules were shaped after the rules of the London Stock Exchange (LSE). In Chapter 7 we will assess how the TSE is again looking to the LSE for a model to create an AIM-like market, as the current exchanges in Japan do not cater for the SME businesses. Similar to the late nineteenth century, which was a time of much-needed change to allow Japan to become competitive with the rest of the world, the deregulation promoted by the Koizumi government encouraged the TSE big bang and looked to foreign exchanges to find a model to incorporate the SME sector, which is often the most innovative. Whether the debate will prove too lively, or whether post-Koizumi governments will be capable of accommodating such a new idea, even if based on historical precedent, remains to be seen.

The LSE-based rules were replaced in 1878 by new rules regulating the exchanges, which stipulated that they had to be organized as joint stock companies licensed under the Ministry of Finance. These exchanges were run privately and were generating profits. Yet, in 1887, a new ordinance was issued according to which exchanges were no longer allowed to be run as stock companies, but were required to be organized as associations of their members. Consequently, existing exchanges had to be liquidated and new ones had to be founded. The result was a great deal of confusion coupled with opposition to these changes. Extensive studies were once again carried out to assess how the European and US exchanges operated, leading to a new Exchange Law in 1893, which superseded the ordinance of 1887. Its enactment provided the possibility of establishing an exchange as a joint stock corporation, while the form of a membership organization also remained viable.[6]

A new role for the Development Bank of Japan

The DBJ began as a reconstruction bank after the Second World War to revitalize the ravaged Japanese economy. It was seen as not having a very important role in recent times, but during the Koizumi administration was brought in as a vehicle not only to deal with NPLs, a critical area of

Japanese economic failure (see Chapter 1), but to promote IPR. These two pillars of economic structural reform and the IP drive were central to the Koizumi administration programme and the DBJ used both to revitalize failing businesses.

The DBJ established a special finance programme for troubled companies to bridge their required financial resources in the supplementary budget for the fiscal year 2001, a year before the first target year set by the government for the removal of NPLs from banks' balance sheets, as most private banks had not been familiar with, and had not been cautious about, this risky banking area.

Intellectual property as collateral

The DBJ set about assisting troubled companies in writing off their debt and revitalizing their businesses in a unique way by using IP as collateral. Loans or guarantees, collateralized by IP, are ways to meet future R&D expense needs through the evaluation of business opportunities derived from such intangible assets. The category includes two kinds of evaluation. One is the use of IP in developing a pipeline to finance future business development and the other is to develop IP to finance new R&D expenses.

Quantitative evaluation to determine what constitutes IP value to be used for collateral is essential. IP is given a present value through a discount method based on projected cash flow that shows that the technical advantage is less important than current cash flow. Potential or future value should not be taken into account and IP that does not produce any cash flow under evaluation will not be available as collateral.

Another essential element is security as collateral. Liquidity and transferability are important for a transferee to continue conducting business with the IP. Security on all necessary IPR for operating a business is also essential. Patents and/or copyrights that provide a business venture with core competence need to be taken as main collateral, while related design rights, trademarks and manuals may be taken as supplementary collateral.

Methodologies to evaluate IP are based on discount cash flow calculations for five years at the most. Projected cash flow at present value may be considered as fair collateral after careful analysis of sales figures calculated by unit price and the number of units, life span, version-up development expenses and timing. The discount rate for present value calculation depends on the track record, market risk or worn-out risk, but currently discount rates of between 10 and 20 per cent are widely applied throughout Japan. Transfer costs such as initial expenditure for human resources and for fixture transfer must also be taken into account and deducted for final assessment.

Great attention must be paid to collateral rights protection, otherwise smooth transfer may be readily eroded. The most important point is to clarify the relationship between multiple patents related to one product. As for the relationship between a fundamental patent and a manufacturing or product patent, there is no allowance for producing a specific product only through using a fundamental patent and it is possible to offend fundamental patent territory with only a manufacturing or product patent. It is also imperative to pay attention to third party rights, such as licensing and joint development. If rent or execution rights are necessary for business, expenditure for those rights should be considered as an additional costing.

The DBJ has provided over 200 loans collateralized by IP in the past nine years and its experience shows that the reality of executing collateral transfer in the event of business failure has been difficult to date. IP owned by troubled enterprises tends to become worthless as salvage value, unless the reason for the failure is not based on the product itself but on a funding gap derived solely from companies' operations. A liquid market has not been developed for IP, even though Techno-mart, a Japanese market for unused IP, works cooperatively with companies.[7] The DBJ finally realized its privatization plans in October 2008, which will be discussed in Chapter 8.

4 Cross-border IP and the fast-tracking of patent applications

Various measures to increase the efficiency of patenting in Japan began in earnest with former Prime Minister Koizumi, since he established the concept of a nation built on IP in his policy speech to the 154th session of the Diet. He was the first incumbent prime minister to do so and Japanese IP practices have been changing rapidly ever since. One of the newest innovations is the concept of a cross-border IP highway, which has been aided by the streamlining of patent applications or the fast-tracking of them during the patent examination system and through the courts. Such changes have allowed some of the very innovative small-scale biotech sectors in Japan to create new competitive products and patent them quickly to protect them from their rivals, especially in the case of the use of newly found plants with medicinal values. Japan, unlike in the past, is also being affected by newly developing, legally binding global agreements that will set the standard for how all drug-based IP will be protected. The IP highway is not the only cross-border IP activity the Japanese have been developing in recent years, but cross-border infringement litigation, especially with its closest East Asian neighbours, is becoming more aggressive and frequent.

The promotion of both efficient and expeditious patent examination, initiated largely during the Koizumi years, has continued and has been accompanied by a reorganization of the patent attorney profession to fit in with the new IP regime.

The rise in the fast-tracking of IP applications

In 2004, a bill to expedite patent examination processes was introduced into the current Diet session. Parallel to this bill and the IP drive being promoted by the Koizumi government, the JPO was employing practical measures to quicken the pace of patent examination. They began this in 2004 with a five-year plan to increase examiners by 100 a year. With 800,000 patents awaiting examinations, the JPO employed additional fixed-term patent examiners.

The JPO moved to eliminate steps that stopped patentees from enforcing their rights from an early stage. This meant that patent applicants would know soon after filing whether or not the results of their research could be patented. This gives companies vital information early on as to whether their product is viable and worth further investment, or whether R&D resources would be better invested in a more promising technical field or endeavour.

In addition to 500 extra patent examiners over the five-year period, the JPO has been expanding the capacity for outsourcing for prior-art searches and deregulating requirements for search organizations. Other incentives offered to improve the patenting environment for applicants include:

- a reduction in fees in the case of examination requests with prior-art search reports prepared by registered search organizations;
- improving the availability of official gazettes published via the internet;
- extending the term of the utility model right from six years to ten years from the filing date;
- converting a utility model registration into a patent application.[1]

The Amari Plan

The Koizumi years, as shown in this book, witnessed a radical promotion of IP that had never been experienced in Japan's history. It was linked to an equally radical economic policy, led by Tanaka Heizo, and the new IP policy (see Chapter 1).

The next Prime Minister after Koizumi, Abe Shinzo, who was forced to resign because of his capitulation to the deeply conservative and damaging forces that Prime Minister Koizumi had kept in check, did attempt to move the reform of the IP system forward. He did this by appointing Amari Akira as the Minister of Economy, Trade and Industry.

On 19 October 2006, the Amari Plan was formulated, which sought to increase the efficiency and expedite patent examination even further than under the Koizumi government. The Amari Plan consisted of four areas and 20 measures. The essence of the Amari Plan is as follows.[2]

The Amari Plan promoted both prompt and global scale acquisition of IPR and a higher level of IP protection. Until the Koizumi years Japan had neglected promotion of its own IP, overlooking inventors at universities and not encouraging inventions to be taken and exploited by business. The bulk of Japanese companies did not have the foresight to see the possibilities of inventions made within their midst let alone remunerate some of their brilliant inventors fairly. This led to the famous employees' right to compensation decision of the Tokyo District Court, whose implications will be dealt with in full in Chapter 5. With such neglect of IP occurring within Japan, an understanding of the importance of, and the ability to detect, much-needed IP globally was a distant reality. Some Japanese companies were using the inventiveness of Taiwan in areas of GPS and telecoms to create new products. As Japanese pharmaceutical companies amassed more wealth through drug monopolies within Japan, they began to realize that to stay competitive it was imperative to buy inventive small companies and spin-outs from abroad. Britain was a target in particular, with its many small companies and spin-outs producing products that were highly inventive and value creating.

The JPO continued its efforts towards streamlining and making patent examination efficient, which is outlined below in relation to the IP highway.

Strategic IP management by companies is also continuing to be promoted, which was established very early on during the Koizumi government with industry, government and university cooperation (see Chapter 1). The continued support for local companies and SMEs in the utilization of IP, which is outlined below, is another feature being carried on by the Amari Plan and the subsequent Fukuda and Aso government.

One of the most important developments in the Japanese IP strategy has been the development of the patent prosecution highway (PPH), which facilitated one of the essential changes under the Koizumi government – an awareness of the importance of globalization and how the Japanese economy could benefit from this. The PPH, with its cross-border nature, has served to expedite; to make Japanese IP more available to the rest of the world; to allow Japanese companies to access more readily potential acquisitions of IP globally; and to assist in the stopping of infringement, which has plagued Japan, especially in relation to China. Below, the first pilot programme of PPH initiated in July 2006 between the USA and Japan is described, as is the Korean PPH, which commenced in Spring 2007.

Special measures to assist SMEs

As SME companies have very particular requirements because of their size, the JPO has introduced a number of supportive systems to cater for their needs, which will expedite their applications. These supportive systems include the following:

- The JPO holds explanatory meetings and seminars concerning IP from the introductory level to strategic acquisition of IPR that meet regional needs and show how to exploit such rights. These sessions are for personnel in SMEs, such as corporate managers and those responsible for R&D, which serves to assist them in exploiting their IPR quickly and efficiently as they are less likely to learn through costly trial and error. SMEs have limited cash and human resources and the JPO assists further in making up for these deficiencies in offering expert individual consultation services on specific matters relating to industrial property rights on a national scale.
- In the regional bureaus of Economy, Trade and Industry dedicated staff members exist to offer consultation services on a regular basis, assisting SME companies in the most expeditious ways to file applications to registration and the actual procedure for filing an application.
- To further support exploitation of IPR and facilitate more rapid patenting, the National Centre of Industrial Property Information (NPIT) sends patent information advisers who are experts in exploiting patent information to many different locations in response to requests by government prefectures. NPIT also provides visit consultation services and workshops for SMEs free of charge.
- To promote efficiency in assessing whether an examination should be requested or not, private search organizations are commissioned by the JPO to perform prior-art searches free of charge for patent applications of both SMEs and individuals prior to requests for examination. The search results are delivered to the applicant by post. This support saves the SME both time and money by being free of charge and determining whether an examination should be requested or not.
- In the event that an examination is necessary, the JPO allows either an exemption or a 50 per cent reduction in examination fees for companies that lack funding, if the company complies with certain requirements, or grants a 50 per cent reduction for SMEs dedicated to R&D activities.

- SME patent applicants or individuals who are already implementing the invention, or are in the process of having an examination or appeal/trial examination, can have their application accelerated if the applicant submits an explanation of the circumstances that necessitate them having an accelerated process.
- The JPO supports more precise acquisition of rights by offering opportunities for applicants or their agents and the examiners or appeal examiners to have meetings in person in order to deepen their understanding of the applications and the technologies/designs.

In addition to interview examinations and interview appeal/trial examinations carried out at the JPO, the JPO examiners or appeal examiners also visit various locations nationwide to conduct circuit examinations, regional interview/appeal/trial examinations and circuit appeal/trials. The JPO also conducts TV interview examinations using a TV conference system installed at the patent offices of the respective Regional Bureaus of Economy, Trade and Industry.

Finally, the JPO allows an exemption from patent annual fees (from the first year to the third year) or a grace period of three years to individuals or companies that are lacking funds, if they comply with certain requirements. Additionally, as mentioned above, the JPO grants a 50 per cent reduction in annual patent fees (from the first to the third year) to SMEs dedicated to R&D.[3]

The new IP highway

Japan began a unique cross-border IP experiment with South Korea about three years ago in which patent applications examined in one country were accepted in the other.

Such agreements were the beginning of far-sighted cross-border agreements or 'IP highways', as they became known. One of the most intractable problems globally for patenting has been the need to patent a product or service in each country of the world, as each country has its own patent rules and, if not patented in one of the countries, the product or service is easier to copy by changing some facet slightly and calling it something else. Patent infringement on a cross-border basis is rife globally.

To rectify this, Japan has established a PPH, first with its neighbour South Korea and the Korean Intellectual Property Office (KIPO), which began on 1 April 2007. The PPH has been successful with South Korea and, since 2003, the JPO, the United States Patent and Trademark Office (USPTO) and the European Patent Office (EPO) (the Trilateral Offices) have worked together in search of exchange projects aimed at promoting the maximum mutual exploitation of search results. These initial projects showed the potential benefit in exploiting the search results of the office of first filing (OFF) to reduce the workload in the office of second filing (OSF) and to improve the quality in cases where the OFF performed the search in advance of the OSF working on the corresponding application. To exploit the search results from the OFF to the OSF is critical for patenting success.

Addressing the time disparity

To address the time disparity in the availability of search results that currently exist among the Trilateral Offices in the case where the JPO is the OFF, the USPTO and the JPO have worked together to create their own PPH. This will provide applicants who file at the JPO with an incentive to file a request for examination at an earlier time and to obtain search and examination results early from the JPO in the case where the JPO is the OFF. Within this framework an applicant whose claims are determined to be allowable/patentable in the OFF can request that the corresponding application filed in the OSF be accelerated with certain conditions being met. This means that the OSF would be able to exploit the search and examination results of the OFF and the applicant may be able to obtain a patent on the corresponding application filed in the OSF faster, since the OSF application is advanced out of turn for examination.

Pilot programmes with the USA and the UK

The USPTO/JPO PPH pilot programme was formerly announced on 22–24 May 2006 at the Trilateral Technical Meeting held in Japan. In the case where the USPTO is the OFF and the US application contains claims that are determined to be allowable/patentable, the US applicant may in turn request accelerated examination in the JPO for the corresponding application filed in the JPO as the OSF and have a special application under the PPH pilot programme. The PPH pilot programme is still on trial with the initial year being extended into 2008.

The latest PPH agreement to be signed in Tokyo on 26 March 2007 has been with the UKPO. Again, the main aim, as with the USPTO, is to improve both the quality and the efficiency of processing applications at both offices. The pilot in the UK will allow patent applicants who have received an examination report by either the UKPO or the JPO to request accelerated examination of a corresponding patent application filed in the other country. Patent applicants will be required to submit search and examination reports prepared by the other patent office so as to qualify for acceleration. This process will allow each office to benefit from work previously done by the other office, which in turn will reduce examination workload and improve the quality of patents.[4]

Goals of the PPH initiative

The aim of the pilot scheme between the UK and Japan is to build on the success to date of the joint PPH being pioneered by the USPTO and the JPO, which will promote greater international efforts to develop work-sharing arrangements on a cross-border basis and will serve eventually to eliminate duplication of effort and allow patent applicants to have their patents protected in more than one country.

The Undersecretary of Commerce for Intellectual Property and Director of the USPTO, Jon Dudas, has noted that 'Streamlining the patent application process benefits all users of the system and reduces costs ... This partnership with our JPO colleagues demonstrates how cooperation by and among offices can result in material improvements for innovators.'[5]

Priority documents have to be filed when applicants wish to claim an earlier application filing date in one patent office based on a prior filing in another. Claiming priority is a valuable tool for businesses wanting to pursue patent rights globally. This is precisely the strategy the Japanese have followed since the Koizumi government to facilitate globalization, in order to revive a flagging economy.

Under the Paris Convention for the Protection of Industrial Property, a treaty that provides a number of important rights for innovators, a patent applicant may file an application in one Paris Convention member country (the priority document) and, within 12 months, file corresponding applications in other member countries, while obtaining the benefit of the first application's filing date. This 12-month period allows applicants to make important decisions about where to file subsequent applications, in order to seek protection for their inventions. Paris Convention filings are a critical component of many applicants' global business and patenting strategies and represent a substantial portion of worldwide patent activity. To obtain the benefit of an earlier filing, however, applicants are generally required to file paper copies of the priority document in each of the later filing offices at their own expense. The new service will allow the USPTO and JPO, with appropriate permission, to obtain electronic copies of priority documents filed with the other office from its electronic image record management system.

To allow the weaknesses and strengths of cross-border systems to be worked out through cross-national cooperation will raise standards that may lead eventually to a universal standard of application. Moving towards a universal IP language, which will most likely be English, will also encourage greater efficiency on a cross-border basis.

Acceleration of the whole examination process can only be beneficial to all countries concerned. For example, in relation to businesses in the UK, the PPH initiative will ensure that patent applications examined by the JPO will be done two years earlier than the average and the quality of the examination will be enhanced by extra work on the application already carried out by the UKPO.

The PPH offers a number of advantages to users. One is the high-quality examination, which facilitates the exploitation of search and examination results, which in turn generates high-quality examination results in the OSF. The PPH also provides quick patent protection in foreign countries, avoiding redundant procedures. The OSF provides an applicant with a simple procedure for accelerated examination. This has in real terms reduced the average waiting period for a patent examination in the JPO from 26 to 2.4 months.[6]

Decrease in average time for application processing

As Figure 4.1a–d shows, the average time from commencement of filing the application to completion has decreased substantially despite a sharp rise in numbers of applications. The average time span for this process is now 10.8 months, when it used to be well over a year. The percentages of IP applications according to type are as follows:

- patents: 38–40 per cent
- copyright: 35 per cent
- unfair competition: 20 per cent
- trademark and design, and others: 20 per cent.

These figures reflect the percentage of each type of application in relation to the total number of applications for all IP.

Cross-border legislation to encourage new drugs

Cross-border cooperation to create new drugs for rare diseases has seen the USA carry out the initial trials, with Japan and the European Union following suit. A similar trend happened with the PPH, although Japan

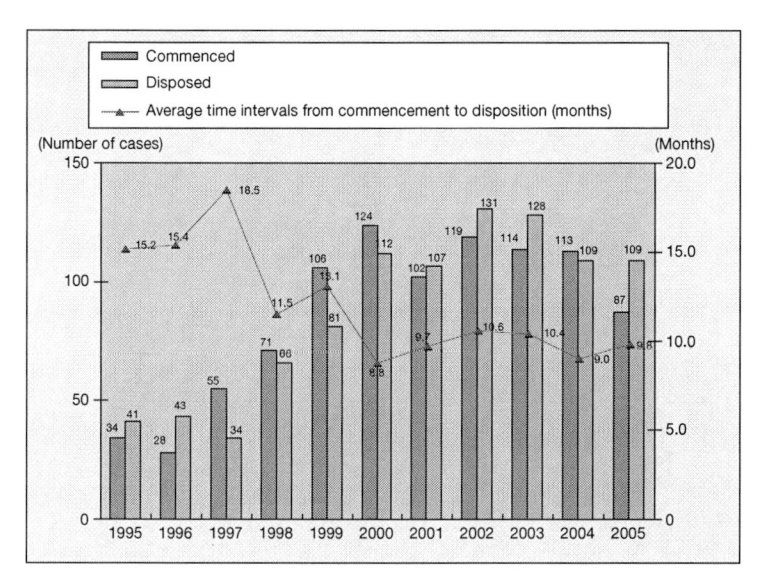

Cross-border IP and the fast-tracking of patent applications 47

(a) Patents

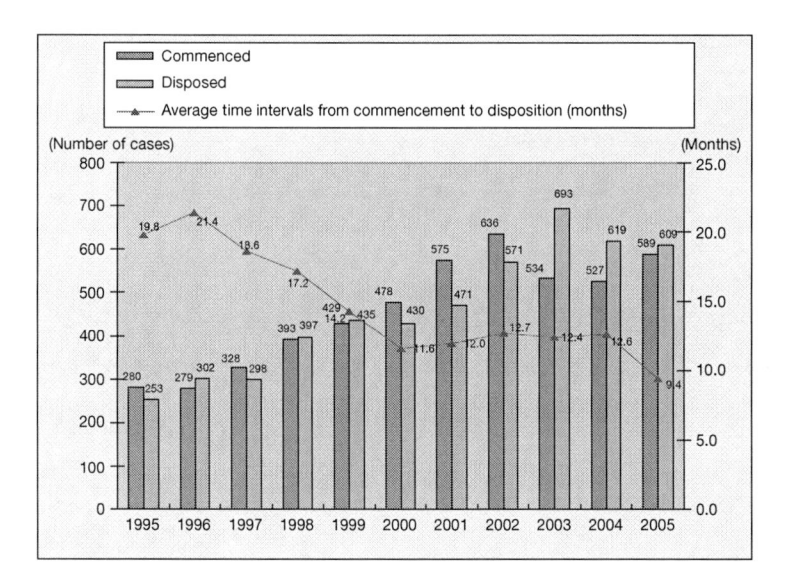

(b) Copyright

Figure 4.1 The number of cases for IPR (First Instance, Tokyo District Court) and the average length required for inquiry. Please note that 'Commenced' refers to the number of new cases accepted, while 'Disposed' refers to the number of cases that have already been settled. The values for 2005 are for those cases settled already.[7]

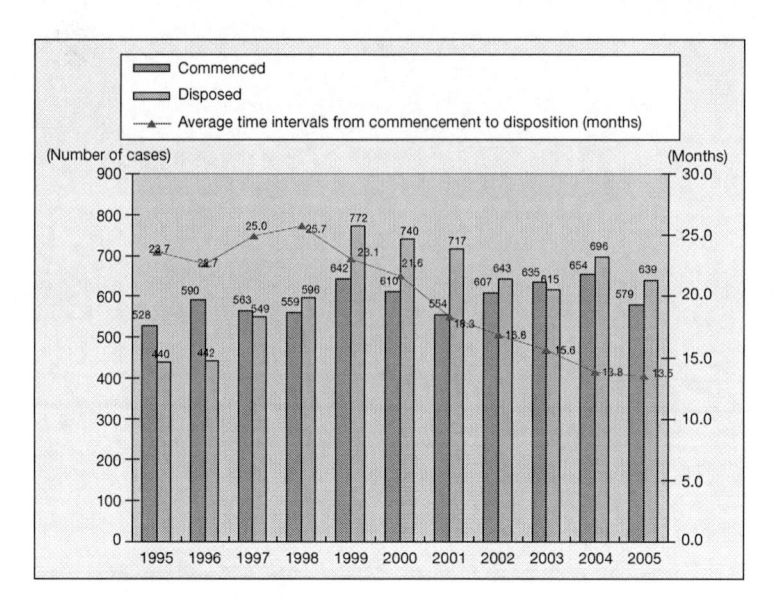

48 *Cross-border IP and the fast-tracking of patent applications*

(c) Unfair competition

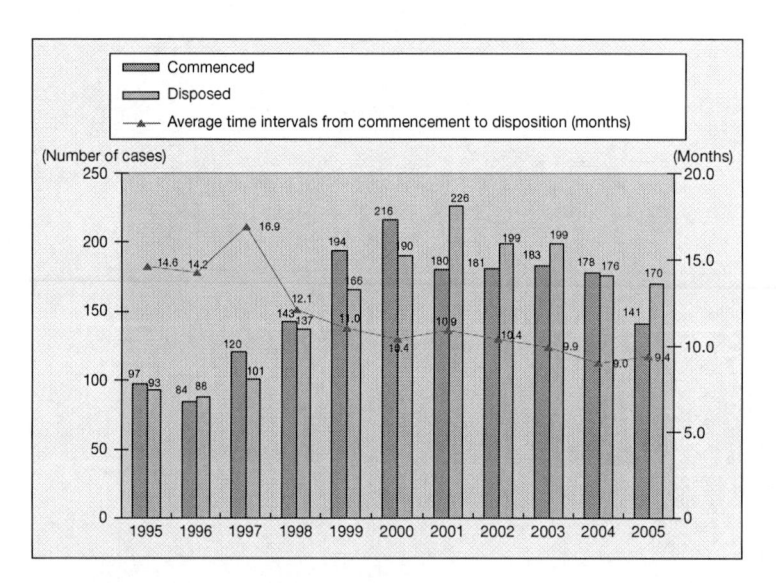

(d) Trademark and design, and others

Figure 4.1 ... continued.

has been in the forefront of leading this trend. The problem was rooted in how new drugs could be created that poorer countries could afford as well.

Some have argued that patent protection is counter to global health for all being achieved. In April 2008, the World Health Organization's Intergovernmental Working Group of Intellectual Property considered reworking global IP rules. The intention is to move away from patenting and increase the role of government in R&D, which is tantamount to nationalizing such research through the back door. Unfortunately such a plan has little to do with the global free market and is having the effect of large pharmaceutical companies losing interest. Japanese large pharmaceutical companies, as in the US and the UK, would react much more favourably to maintaining a profit while lowering research costs. Japanese pharmaceutical companies hold enormous capital reserves and in their bid to globalize and expand their patented range of drugs have been supporting spin-outs in Japan, which are producing a wide range of innovative drugs, such as hitherto unknown plants for nutritional purposes. They have also been buying up small innovative English companies that produce innovative drugs.

Therefore, in place of adopting the governmental approach that dismantles patents, Japan has introduced legislation similar to that of the USA. This legislation is based on the US Orphan Drug Act (ODA). The ODA offers tax credits, seven years of market exclusivity and consultation with the Food and Drug Administration (FDA) staff to companies that are willing to create drug treatments for rare diseases that only affect small populations. Since the bill was enacted in 1983, the average annual number of new drugs for rare diseases was 12 times that of the previous decade.

Recently, in 2006, researchers at Duke University in the USA introduced a transferable voucher system for the developers of drugs for neglected diseases, which became law as part of the FDA's Amendment Acts of 2007. This has resulted in companies who develop drugs for neglected and rare diseases receiving a voucher for the FDA's 'priority review'. This means that a fast-tracking of FDA evaluation takes place in about six months, which is much more rapid than the standard evaluation of one year. Companies that will be producing a drug that will be greatly in demand, by getting their product to the market a year early, can save hundreds of millions of dollars in additional revenue that can then be put into R&D. Smaller companies can also auction their vouchers to the highest bidder, which will also raise much-needed additional funds for research.

Beginning September 2008, vouchers were available for treatments of 16 neglected diseases or for any other infectious diseases for which there are no current drugs available in developing markets. It should not be long before Japan enters this phase of the latest ODA legislation as the Japanese population is becoming disproportionately elderly, with rare diseases increasing, and Japan has been a supporter through the Japan International Cooperation Agency (JICA) of improving the lives of those in developing countries. This example also shows how IP can be used flexibly within a free market system and to good effect.[8]

Cross-border cooperation against infringement

In recent years, trade relationships between Japan and its neighbours have been marked by allegations and litigation. Japanese companies have initiated wide-ranging legal and other measures against East Asian businesses. Many lawsuits deal with South Korean patent infringement, including:

- Toshiba's allegations against Hyundai on flash storage;
- Matsushita's complaints against LG for plasma displays – LG electronics products have now been deprived of access to the Japanese market;
- Fujitsu's criticism of Samsung.

Another recent example is Sharp's lawsuit against a Taiwanese company for LCD patent infringement.

Intellectual property rights in electronics products

Intellectual property rights (IPR), especially in the electronics product arena, are regarded as being central to sustaining Japanese economic recovery through the development of new-generation products. To support this, Japanese companies have banded together to unleash concerted patent protection action against their East Asian competitors. A number of Japanese electronic and mechanical producers have demanded a cessation of infringements by, and economic compensation from, Chinese, South Korean and Taiwanese enterprises.

Twenty-one Japanese manufacturers in China have been working in tandem to investigate and lodge complaints against Chinese companies.

Many Japanese companies – including Toshiba, Canon, NEC, Hitachi, Matsushita, Sony, Sharp and Olympus – have also developed in-house IPR teams to trace and deal with IP infringements.

Cooperation between Japan and China

To tackle the infringement problems more directly and aggressively, according to a report in JiJi Press, Japan and China have agreed to cooperate more fully in prosecuting those who are making illegal copies of Japanese goods in China.

In 2005 a series of meetings were held between Chinese IPR officials and a Japanese delegation led by the former Chairman of Honda Motor Company, Mr Munekuni Yoshihide. Following these meetings, Japan's International Intellectual Property Protection Forum proposed in June 2005 that Japan would assist in instituting a number of anti-counterfeiting measures. These include:

- sending Japanese experts to China to hold seminars showing Chinese enforcement agents how to distinguish counterfeit products from the genuine articles;
- providing past examples of illegally copied goods.

Mr Munekuni told a press conference that he believed China was making progress in inhibiting the production of counterfeit goods because government ministries are working closer together to improve enforcement.

Within Japan, universities are beginning to hold Chinese company law and basic law courses, so expertise can be developed to stem the increasing tide of infringement cases.

Future global battlegrounds

The next battleground to see Japanese businesses take action against Chinese competitors will involve Japanese digital camera makers. This is because unlicensed technologies of Japanese origin are embedded in low-cost digital cameras that are made in China. To not take the Chinese infringers to task would mean losing ground as the rate of innovation of these products is so rapid.

Litigation has also been brewing in the automotive sector. Nissan and Honda have established sections in their Chinese operations to deal with patent infringement cases, and Toyota is thinking about following the other car manufacturers' example.

Bringing infringers to court

The task of the experts in Japanese-funded enterprises in China will be to collect evidence of patent infringements and counterfeited products. This evidence will be used to encourage the Chinese departments of Public Security, Industry and Commerce to enforce existing IP law against Chinese enterprises that infringe. Contrary to the traditional behaviour of the Japanese, which avoids confrontation and litigation, these experts will use the evidence to bring Chinese businesses to court.

After joining the WTO, China has made efforts to protect IP rights. The recent examples of court rulings outlined below are giving Japanese companies hope that enforcement is becoming tighter:

- Between 2000 and November 2004, Chinese courts on a nationwide basis made rulings in 2,171 cases of illegal production; 1,948 Chinese individuals were charged with infringement offences during the first trial.
- Between 2002 and October 2004, another 1,271 cases of illegal production and the sale of counterfeited and poor-quality products were brought to trial.
- The Chinese prosecutor's office also arrested 2,462 people in 1,539 infringement cases, and indicted 2,491 people in 1,500 cases, between 2000 and November 2004.
- The Supreme People's Court has from the year 2000 published 25 legal explanation documents about IPR court cases.

The two sample cases below – taken from December 2004 – show the efficacy of the Chinese courts in upholding Japanese evidence of counterfeiting or trademark infringement:

- A Beijing court ruled in favour of Honda Motor Company in a trademark lawsuit against a Chinese company using the name 'Hongda' and decreed that the latter must desist from using their name and pay damages to Honda. The Beijing No. 2 Intermediate People's Court ordered Chongqing Lifan Industry Group Co., a private motorcycle maker, to pay 1.47 million yuan (about £92,000) in damages to Japan's largest motorcycle manufacturer.

- Ricoh, the Japanese electronics company, reached an out-of-court settlement in December 2004 with Taiwanese company CMC Magnetics, after appealing to a California federal court concerning CMC's infringement of an optic data recorder patent.[9]

New directions for Japanese patent attorneys

In Japan, since the Koizumi government, nothing is sacred – not the JPO nor the profession of specialized Japanese patent attorneys known as *benrishi*. Not since the Meiji Era have there been so many changes to the law concerning *benrishi*. With the recent emphasis on patenting and IP there has also been a pressing need for more qualified *benrishi* at different levels of qualification, because to become a fully qualified *benrishi* is very difficult.

Every practising attorney in Japan is required to be a member of the Japan Patent Attorneys Association (JPAA). The JPAA is overseen by the JPO and is operational through fees collected from its members. Its annual budget of roughly 1.9 billion yen (about 12 million euros), including associated organizations (more than 30 committees and several institutes such as the Educational Institute), supports a staff of about 50. *Benrishi* numbered 6,800 as of November 2006 and sole practitioners accounted for 33 per cent of the total.

In 2002, an additional qualification was added – the *Fuki Benrishi*, or 'Patent Attorney with Addendum to Registration'. These *benrishi* can represent clients only jointly with attorneys at law (*bengoshi*) and only in specific types of litigation, including patent, trademark, design, utility model and circuit layout rights infringement, in addition to specific acts of unfair competition. This qualification is awarded after 45 hours of course work and a successful examination. The pass rate for the examination is approximately 60–70 per cent and, as of June 2006, roughly 1,500 had attained this qualification.

The importance of the *benrishi* underpinning the IP drive under the Koizumi government was highlighted in a statement by Shimosaka Sumiko in 2004, when she was President of the JPAA. She outlined a number of key areas for the JPAA to concentrate on, including the problems of counterfeiting and infringement of IP in Asia; participating more in international conferences; and working together with more international IP organizations. This increasingly international outlook mirrors the overall emphasis of the Japanese in moving towards a globalized economy and an added awareness that, to be competitive once more, Japan must acknowledge the impact the world has on its economy and vice versa.

Shimosaka further noted that paramount is the training of *benrishi* to have the expertise to cope with the new complex reforms and laws, mentioned above and below, which allow them to represent clients jointly and equally with the *bengoshi*.[10]

Changes to the law concerning patent attorneys

In November 2006, a summary of changes was put in draft by a subcommittee of the Industrial Structure Committee organized by the Ministry of Economy, Industry and Trade, which oversees the JPO. The new law, which became effective in 2007, initiated a programme of further training responsibilities for *benrishi* in Japan. Mandatory training for newly registered *benrishi* is of three months' duration with e-learning and schooling on Saturdays. Additional training of 70 hours over five years has also been demanded. The inclusion of foreign filing work as one of the stated job responsibilities has ensued for *benrishi* under the Patent Attorneys Law. There is also further scope for expansion of possible professional work under the Unfair Competition Prevention Law. Patent attorneys are being compelled to disclose information concerning their specializations and other details relevant to a case. What has not changed is the rule enacted under the 2000 Patent Attorneys Law that no attorney at law can constitute a member of the *benrishi* corporation. The corporation continues to receive work from clients and it is the corporation, not individual *benrishi*, that may represent clients before the JPO and courts. This attitude derives from the collective nature of Japan and its tradition in which institutions work with institutions not individuals.

Another expansion of the remit of *benrishi* is that of filing a petition or factual information at the customs office for injunction orders against importation of products suspected of IP infringement. As mentioned above, Japanese companies have been exerting pressure and acting to strengthen customs procedures to curtail infringement. In these cases of customs, however, *benrishi* cannot represent the defence side, which comprises the importers. *Benrishi* may make representations before specialized arbitration/mediation organizations, especially for matters related to industrial property, circuit layout and specific acts of unfair competition. Other organizations include the Japan IP Arbitration Centre, founded in 1998, which is operated jointly by the JPAA and the Japan Federation of Bar Associations and the Japan Commercial Arbitration Association.

Finally, to become a patent attorney a person has to pass the patent attorney examination, which constitutes about 84 per cent of *benrishi*, while only about 5 per cent are also *bengoshi*. Patent attorneys may also be drawn from the ranks of JPO examiners who have seven years or more of experience as examiners or appeal examiners at the JPO. The latter constitute about 10 per cent of patent attorneys, while about 1 per cent are allowed to become patent attorneys for a variety of reasons. A foreign national can be a Japanese patent attorney and not be required to reside in Japan.[11]

5 Changes to the Patent Court and employees' rights to compensation

Establishment of IP courts

The establishment of the Intellectual Property Division of the Tokyo High Court and Tokyo District Court occurred in 1950 and 1961 respectively, while in Osaka the Osaka District Court was established in 1964 and the Osaka High Court in 1990. However, it was after the collapse of the 'bubble-economy' in 1990 that the promotion of IP and patenting was viewed as an essential measure to revitalize the Japanese economy. This led in June 2001 to the Justice System Reform Council publishing their recommendations in *Strengthening of a Comprehensive Response to Cases Related to Intellectual Property Rights*, which proposed that IPR is one of the most important subjects within the context of civil justice reform, coupled with increased professionalism in IP case resolution.

As outlined in Chapter 1, the then Prime Minister Koizumi provided the necessary impetus, with his General Policy Speech in February 2002 and through the idea of an intellectual property nation, with the Basic Law on Intellectual Property coming into force in March 2003 and an Intellectual Property Policy Headquarters established in the cabinet. It was the headquarters that adopted the Strategic Programme for the Creation, Protection and Exploitation of Intellectual Property in July 2003, in which it recommended the establishment of the IP High Court to reinforce the idea that IP was one of the top national priorities and the dispute resolution function. After much debate between the business community, the legal profession and the government, the Secretariat of the Office for the Promotion of Justice Reform worked on a bill and, in June 2004, the Law for Establishing the IP High Court was enacted. On 1 April 2005, the IP High Court was established as a 'special branch' of the Tokyo High Court. This meant that, after 50 years, the IP High Court would be the sole court to deal with IP issues within the Tokyo High Court system.

Organization of the IP courts

The bespoke IP Court consists of a particular structure, including a Litigation Department and the IP High Court Secretariat. Chief Judge Shinohara has the greatest seniority and is supported by a number of highly qualified judges, judicial research officials of IP cases, court clerks and court secretaries. Expert commissioners may also be involved in IP cases as part-time officials on a case-by-case basis.

There is a panel of three judges or the Grand Panel of five judges at the IP Court who conduct proceedings and give judgments. The Grand Panel serves when there are particularly important issues in a case or an expeditious settlement of unified judicial opinions is required.

Judicial research officials are assigned by the order of judges to conduct technical research required by court proceedings, to assist in making judgments relating to patents, utility models and other intellectual property issues. According to Article 92-8 of the Code of Civil Procedure, enacted in April 2005, judicial research officials, with permission of the judges, may ask questions of the parties involved in the case during oral argument or on other relevant occasions in order to clarify aspects of the case.

Court clerks attend and record proceedings, manage the progress of the proceedings, prepare and keep case files, assist judges in researching relevant laws and regulations in addition to judicial precedents, and carry out other services in proceedings as provided by law. Court secretaries, on the other hand, provide judicial administrative services.

Expert commissioners or advisers, as described in further detail below, are an important resource for the IP High Court and become involved by decision of the court to assist judges in providing information and explanations of technical knowledge in cases where their expertise is necessary to clarify issues of the case or to facilitate progress in the proceedings according to Article 92-2 of the Code of Civil Procedure. Expert Commissioners are appointed by the Supreme Court as part-time officials, from among experts such as university professors and researchers of public research institutes who have expertise in scientific fields.

Changes in jurisdiction

The IP High Court has 18 judges and 11 research officers. To facilitate expeditious hearing procedures in all the patent and other technical cases in Japan, an amendment was made to the Code of Civil Procedure that had been enforced on 1 April 2004. The amendment has granted exclusive jurisdiction to the Tokyo and Osaka District Courts over all cases relating to patent rights, utility model rights, circuit layout utilization rights and authors' rights in Japan.

The Tokyo District Court, therefore, has exclusive jurisdiction over such litigation in the eastern part of Japan and the Osaka District Court over the western part of Japan. As all cases under the jurisdiction of the Tokyo High Court can be heard by the IP High Court, it has exclusive jurisdiction nationwide over appeals from the Tokyo and Osaka Courts regarding patent and other technical cases, while the IP divisions of the Tokyo and Osaka District Courts continue to hear most cases in the first instance.

For the sake of speed, cases relating to design rights, trademark rights, copyrights (excluding program copyrights) and unfair competition prevention law may, for eastern Japan, be brought before the Tokyo District Court and those under the jurisdiction of a district court in western Japan be brought before the Osaka District Court.[1]

Invalidity defence

An amendment of the Patent Law through the enactment of Article 104-3 on 1 April 2005 meant that a defendant could raise the invalidity defence in patent and other IP litigations. The Japanese Supreme Court decided in the Kilby case on 11 April 2000 that, if a patent is apparently invalid, a defendant can make a defence regarding the abuse of rights in patent infringement litigation. This is called an apparent invalidity defence and before this decision it was difficult for this defence to be adopted. This new law, therefore, changed the apparent invalidity defence into an invalidity defence, so that whether validity is apparent or not is no longer an issue.

In actuality, this amendment had little impact on the practice of district courts in infringement litigations because they had already been deciding validity of patents based on the Kilby decision without waiting for decisions to be made in invalidation petitions by the JPO. The amendment has authorized a court to decide the validity of a patent in infringement lawsuits for total and single-round resolutions of patent disputes. It does not request the accused infringer to apply for the invalidation petition to the JPO.

According to the JPO, allegations of 'abuse of a patent right' have been raised as a defence more frequently in infringement litigations after the Kilby decision. The defence was alleged in 2004 in up to 80 per cent of infringement lawsuits and in 60 per cent of invalidation petitions, which are simultaneously applied before the Boards of the JPO.

The creation of Article 104-3 does not change the significance of invalidation decisions by the Boards of the JPO, since they can invalidate a patent right itself. If anything, the role of the invalidation hearing in infringement litigations has become even more important.

An additional provision, Article 104-3(2), has been added to the original Article 104-3(1) in the Patent Law in order to prevent its abuse. This added article states that, if the accused infringer submits the grounds for the invalidation for the purpose of causing undue delay in the proceedings, the court may dismiss such invalidation defence. However, concern that this provision may be abused by parties listing as many grounds as possible for invalidation has proved unfounded.

In quite a number of cases, where an invalidation hearing and infringement litigation with respect to the same patent are pursued at the same time in a district court and before a Board of the JPO, the defendant of infringement litigation often alleges as a defence that a patent is invalid based on Article 104-3 of the Patent Law, in addition to applying an invalidation petition before a Board of the JPO or filing a lawsuit against Board decisions of the JPO to the IP High Court. This means that situations may arise in which a lawsuit against a Board decision is pending before the IP High Court while infringement litigation or its appeal with respect to the same patent is pending before a district court or the IP High Court.

In the case where a lawsuit against the Board decision and an appeal against the district court decision involving the same patent are concurrently pending before the IP High Court, it is often the case in the High Court that the same panel hears both cases depending on the willingness of the parties and the progress in the cases.

It is of interest to note that actual practice varies among the district courts and that judges of the Osaka District Court have a tendency to stay infringement lawsuits while awaiting the decision of the IP High Court on the validity of a patent if the Osaka District Court has differing views from the Board decisions concerning validity of the patent. Judges of the Tokyo District Court rarely stay infringement proceedings.

Expert advisory system

From a comparative law perspective and to further understanding of the Japanese judicial system, the expert commissioners system introduced in 2004 is a unique system that offers highly professional judicial services within the area of highly developed, specialized and advanced technology.

Expert advisers are appointed by the Supreme Court on a part-time basis as staff for a two-year term. They are chosen from leading experts in a number of technical fields drawn from the ranks of private companies, *benrishi*, researchers from public organizations and university professors. There are approximately 182 expert commissioners who have been appointed to date and who are considered suitable for such a job. The role of these expert commissioners is to serve as neutral and fair advisers to the court.

Within the proceedings they explain background to or significance of the invention based on both evidence and arguments submitted by parties to the court. The explanations offered by the expert advisers in the proceedings are not viewed as evidence per se, but assist the court in deepening its understanding of the intricacies of the actual invention and other references involved in the case, which facilitates a decision based on evidence. The combination, therefore, of research officials' daily support and expert commissioners' case-by-case assistance is giving the Tokyo and Osaka District Courts and the IP High Court greater levels of expertise to deal with highly technical cases.

The expert advisory system has ushered in a number of positive effects on the judiciary. The explanation by expert advisers to a judge brings higher-quality decisions. Such explanations allow judges to deepen their understanding of the background and provide a total picture of an invention, which helps the judges to piece together the different parts of submitted evidence. They also serve to clear up the questions and doubts the judges may have, giving them increased confidence to make a decision.

Protective orders and patent infringement

Japanese courts do not have a discovery system, but the courts can order a party to submit documents necessary to prove the structure or disposition of the accused products or processes and documents to calculate the amount of damages in the procedure of the patent infringement litigation, if the courts think it necessary to decide the case.

According to Article 105, the court cannot order the party to submit such documents if there are sufficient reasons to refuse to do so. In such cases, for example trade secrets, it has been difficult for the court to reach expeditiously a final conclusion in patent infringement litigation.

The protective order system was established by an amendment to the Patent Law and other IP laws enacted on 1 April 2005, to ensure that litigation proceeds swiftly. The other IP laws include the Design Law, the Trademark Law, the Unfair Competition Prevention Law and the Copyright Law.

This means that, if a defendant has sufficient reason to refuse disclosure of documents because of a trade secret, the court can order the parties and attorneys not to reveal any trade secrets to a third party and to use the information only for prosecution of the patent litigation, and can order the defendant to submit documents.

The Japanese culture avoids confrontation and intrusiveness, which is especially the case in relation to money and business matters, so, while the protective order system has been adopted in England and the USA for many years, Japan resisted its introduction vigorously. The Japanese industrial world, however, realized that, to be globally competitive, they had to encourage the courts to adopt such a procedure, which quickens IP litigation and offers strong protection of IP rights in line with Japan becoming a nation based on IPR.

However, the intrinsic reluctance of Japanese companies to actually use such a protective order may be seen in the minimal use of the order. Parties are cautious because the order imposes a heavy and broad obligation on the party receiving the order, which is often applied more broadly than the particular case and causes the party to become involved in criminal sanctions that cause a severe loss of face. This system is also viewed as lacking because it does not apply to employee invention litigation.[2]

Importance of the employees' rights to compensation judgment

A serious challenge to Japan's economy and its global competitiveness has been its treatment of its inventors, who were regarded as simply part of a team and who were remunerated poorly while the company reaped massive rewards from their creativity. Not content to be treated with derision, a number of the most influential inventors left for the USA and elsewhere in order to be given acknowledgement and commensurate remuneration for their inventive genius. For many years the Japanese did not appear to realize that the old adage of 'hammer down the nail that sticks up' was inappropriate in a globally competitive world, where the nail that sticks up is the extra value created to allow innovative products and services to be developed that would create global demand.

What woke up Japan collectively in the business and judicial world was the hitherto largely unheard-of case of an inventor suing his company from California for proper remuneration for his groundbreaking invention and a visionary judgment that had repercussions for employers and employee relations on a global scale.

The blue light-emitting diode

The now legendary judgment meted out by Judge Shitara Ryuichi, Presiding Judge of the Intellectual Property Division of the Tokyo District Court, created repercussions around the world concerning employees' rights to compensation and is considered one of the most famous judicial decisions in Japan. Prior to this judgment, employees' rights to compensation had not changed substantially in law since the Patent Law of 1960. Employees of both companies and businesses had been reluctant to invent, or to license their inventions, because of the poor relations between business and universities, with the latter not only not being entitled historically to own their own IP but being remunerated poorly. This resulted in inventions stagnating and emigration to the USA, where remuneration was high and quality facilities and honours were lavished upon Japanese inventors. Equally worrying to the Japanese business world and economy were the high settlements being granted by the Tokyo High Court in 2004. This led to the more pressing problem of how to deal with the flood of compensation claims by current or former employees that followed the Nakamura Shuji case. Success by others in obtaining adequate compensation and comparisons with colleagues in the USA and the UK led only to growing resentment on the part of inventors. Japanese inventors saw how well Nakamura was compensated and witnessed further employee success when they travelled abroad.

Nakamura Shuji was instrumental in the development of a two-way light-emitting diode (LED) semiconductor, which glows blue when electricity is passed through it. The invention (also known as the 404 patent) was estimated to net Nichia Corporation, his employer, at least 120.8 billion yen in profits through its exclusive ownership rights up to October 2010. The Tokyo District Court itself decided that half of the sales amount was due to an exclusive right of the two-way invention; that the profit due to this patented invention would be calculated by multiplying half of the sales amount by 20 per cent, which is a hypothetical running royalty rate of the invention; and that $US 1.09 billion was the amount of profit that Nichia obtained from the two-way invention. In Section 4 of Article 35 it states that the amount of the aforementioned appropriate cost should be decided by considering the amount of the profit that the employer will obtain from the invention and by considering the degree of the contribution by the employer to the making of the invention. The District Court also found and took into account that Mr Nakamura did create this invention himself and not as part of a team, which is the usual context in which an invention is described, as sole inventors are always deemed to be part of a team.

The employer bought the machine for $US 2,700,000, but was not very cooperative to Mr Nakamura because the Nichia representative negatively assessed the possibilities of this blue LED, even ordering Mr Nakamura to halt his research on the invention. The Tokyo District Court, based on the judgment of Judge Shitara, calculated that Nichia should pay Nakamura half of the potential profit, amounting to 60.43 billion yen, based on the premise that the contribution by the employer to this invention was only 50 per cent, but since Nakamura had asked for 20 billion yen the court ordered Nichia to pay that amount as compensation for his invention. Nichia had paid only 20,000 yen for the assignment of this invention in the past. Thus, when the Tokyo District Court ordered Nichia to pay about 20 billion yen as a part of the reasonable remuneration, it amounted to one million times the amount that Nichia had paid in the past for the assignment of this invention. The Tokyo District Court had estimated approximately 60 billion yen as a reasonable remuneration for this invention, but the plaintiff demanded in this litigation only 20 billion yen. In Japan, the courts cannot order a defendant to pay an amount higher than the plaintiff demanded in the litigation.

In January 2005, Nakamura settled with Nichia Corporation for 844 million yen ($US 8 million) as the Tokyo High Court overturned the decision of the District Court, which had initially awarded the inventor 20 billion yen ($US 187 million). The Japanese Business Federation was relieved, as were other businesses and employer organizations around the world. The Tokyo District Court, however, found that Mr Nakamura was solely responsible for the invention, contrary to the statement issued by Nichia that the invention was a joint effort. As mentioned above, Nichia had bought the invention for $US 2,700,000 and had assessed in a negative light the potential value of the blue LED, even ordering Mr Nakamura to cease research on their tremendously important invention at one point. This was why the contribution to the employer was deemed to be only 50 per cent.

> It is very difficult to legislate for the lack of vision by institutions and employers. It also appears that, without such a ruling by the Tokyo District Court, inventors would have confirmed in their minds that they will never be remunerated properly in Japan and they would become demotivated and then emigrate elsewhere.[3]

The Nakamura case was not an isolated one. The day before the Nakamura ruling, the Tokyo High Court ordered electronics company Hitachi to pay their ex-employee Yonezawa Seiji what was then a record 163 million yen ($US 1.5 million) for his contribution to optical disc technology. Prior to this judgment, Hitachi had compensated Mr Yonezawa with only 2.3 million yen for early-stage DVD technology. In a landmark case in 2004, *Olympus v. Tanaka*, the Supreme Court made it clear that inventors can sue their companies for larger shares of the profits resulting from a successful invention, irrespective of employee agreements and internal rules. This appeared to provide the courts with total discretion to allocate size of reward, which had been evidenced by the Yonezawa, Nakamura and many other subsequent cases. This resulted in litigation over IP rising to over 700 cases in 2003 from virtually none over the decade before that time, while there were 602 complaints filed with the Tokyo High Court concerning decisions made by the JPO, including 421 over patent rights. In Japan, a country traditionally averse to litigation, these events have marked a significant change.[4]

A new trend in employees' invention compensation

One of the most neglected aspects of the Nakamura case, and one that requires further explanation as it has had implications for subsequent cases, is the reason why the remuneration awarded by the High Court was restricted to roughly one hundredth of the original award. To understand this, an explanation of the outline of the Patent Law with respect to employee inventions is required.

- Paragraph 1 of Article 35 of the Japanese Patent Law states that, where an employee has obtained a patent right relating to the employee's duty, the employer shall have a non-exclusive licence to the patent.
- Paragraph 3 of Article 35 provides that the employee has the right to be paid a reasonable remuneration when he assigns to his employer a patent or right to obtain a patent for the employee's invention in accordance with the contract or employment regulations.
- Before the 2004 amendment of the Japanese Patent Law, Paragraph 4 of Article 35 stated that the amount of the aforementioned reasonable remuneration shall be decided by considering the amount of the profit that the employer shall obtain from the invention and by considering the degree of the contribution by the employer to the making of the invention.

- The Japanese Supreme Court decided in the Olympus case on 22 April 2003 that an employee who assigned his right to obtain a patent for the employee's invention may claim the difference, in the case when the amount paid by the employer falls short of the amount of reasonable remuneration provided for in Paragraphs 3 and 4 of Article 35 of the Patent Law.
- Paragraph 4 of Article 35 was amended in 2004 and Paragraphs 4 and 5 were newly created, but the amended Paragraphs 4 and 5 of Article 35 are applied only to employees' inventions assigned after 1 April 2005.
- Consequently, Paragraph 4 of Article 35 as it was before the 2004 amendment will still be applied to almost all the cases that are filed to the court over the next few decades.

The essence of the opinion of the Tokyo High Court is as follows:

> The amount of remuneration should comply with the object of the Patent Law, which is to 'encourage inventions' and 'contribute to the development of industry'. In other words, reasonable remuneration for the assignment of the right to obtain a patent for an employee invention should be both sufficient to provide an incentive for employees to invent, and at the same time be such that companies can overcome harsh economic conditions and international competition and develop. This reasonable remuneration is naturally of a different nature to the amount of profit the joint operators of companies subject to various risks receive under favourable economic conditions.

In the following, Judge Shitara explains the High Court decision that was necessary to provide a balance to this case, which would be used as a precedent for future cases.

Implications of the Nakamura Shuji decision

The employer has to face various risks in his business and has to bear the liability and risk of loss incurred, but the employee does not have to face the risk of loss and does not have to bear any liability incurred by the employer's business. High risk and high return or no risk and low return, therefore, is the defining principle. This idea is central to the opinion of the High Court when deciding the rate of an employee's contribution to the making of an invention.

In contrast to the Tokyo District Court's decision that an employee's contribution rate is 50 per cent, the Tokyo High Court decided that the contribution rate is 5 per cent. Currently, this Tokyo High Court opinion has had great influence over all the other cases and has been evaluated as one of the leading precedents for reasonable remuneration in Japanese practice. Five per cent continues to be the figure that is most frequently used in Japanese practice as an employee's contribution to an invention.

Judge Shitara explains that another reason why the remuneration awarded by the High Court was restricted is that the employer, Nichia, entered into free comprehensive cross-licensing agreements with two other rival companies in 2002. Besides these two there are no other rival companies in the world. Therefore, until the cross-licensing agreements were made, Nichia had enjoyed the exclusive right to practise the 404 patent. But after the free comprehensive cross-licensing agreements were made, each of these two rival companies could practise this invention.

Before Nichia made cross-licensing agreements and while it still enjoyed the exclusive right to practise the 404 patent, the profit the employer earned from this patented invention could be calculated on the sales basis of Nichia. For example, the profit earned from this invention was calculated by the High Court, by assuming half of Nichia's sales amount arose because of the exclusive rights to the 404 patent and by multiplying the hypothetical royalty rate of 10 or 7 per cent on those sales. However, after the free comprehensive cross-licensing agreements were made, Nichia could not enjoy that exclusivity.

The amount, therefore, of the royalty to be earned from the license agreements formed the basis of calculation of the amount of the profit to be earned from the 404 patent for the term after the cross-license agreements, but no royalty has been paid from the licensee to Nichia in the aforementioned free cross-license agreement.

In the District Court judgment, the court decided the profit earned from the patented invention, assuming that Nichia would enjoy the exclusive rights for the entire period of the 404 patent. However, as Judge Shitara explains, the High Court opinion did not adopt this calculation method due to the aforementioned free cross-license agreement. The Tokyo High Court calculated the profit to be earned from the 404 patent for the term from the conclusion of the cross-license agreements until the expiration of the patent in a very limited way.

The latest Supreme Court decision

On 17 October 2006, a Supreme Court decision was made in relation to the aforementioned Hitachi case. The Supreme Court held that:

1   In this case, the assignment contract for the employee's invention was made between the Japanese company and Japanese employee in Japan. So the law that governs the legal effect of this assignment contract for the right to obtain a patent in this case is Japanese law.
2   With respect to the aforementioned assignment contract between employer and employee for employees' rights to obtain a foreign patent, Article 35 of the Japanese Patent Law is not to be applied directly, but will be applied analogically.
3   The Court concluded that the employer has to pay the employee reasonable remuneration for the assignment of the employee's right to obtain a Japanese patent and a foreign patent.
4   The Supreme Court rejected the final appeal by Hitachi. Therefore, the judgment of the Tokyo High Court ordering Hitachi to pay about 160 million yen as a reasonable remuneration was upheld.
5   Judge Shitara notes that the Supreme Court is the final court only for important legal issues. In the Hitachi case, the Supreme Court decided the legal issues – first, the governing law and, second, applicability of Article 35 of the Patent Law to the assignment contract for the employee's rights to obtain a foreign patent. Yet, the Supreme Court did not make decisions regarding other matters, such as whether the 160 million yen that the Tokyo High Court ordered Hitachi to pay is reasonable remuneration under Article 35 of the Japanese Patent Law.[5]

The laws enacted and action taken by the Tokyo District Court, accompanied by changes to the Articles mentioned above, have been effective as employees' rights to compensation cases decreased to only ten a year in 2007.

6 Changes in Japanese corporate governance

Since the family-run *zaibatsu*, such as that of the Mitsui group, which began in the sixteenth century, Japanese companies have been interconnected through cross-shareholdings but through the family. After the Second World War and the American dissolution of the family-operated monopolies, which broke anti-trust law, a new form of large conglomerate emerged. This is the *sogo shosha/keiretsu*, which is a complex institution that is not family owned and has its own banks and internal financial systems.

Commercial law in Japan, which has governed corporations since the Meiji Era, had remained unchanged until the Koizumi government initiated and carried out widespread reforms. Central to the traditional practice of corporate governance, which kept out foreigners except at the extreme margins of the business world, has been a system of cross-shareholdings, but with the impetus to become more globally competitive new laws have been introduced to promote transparency and accountability in the Japanese corporate sector. Cross-shareholding has seen a decline as a defence mechanism, being replaced by other measures, including the 'poison pill' (see p. 77), which has been used to defend Japanese companies from hostile takeovers by either other Japanese or foreign companies or via the recent triangular mergers.[1]

Horizontal and vertical groupings

Japanese corporate groups can be divided into two different forms, one horizontal and one vertical. The former is based on the old *zaibatsu* family-owned grouping. Today these companies, such as Mitsui and Mitsubishi, hold at least 25 per cent of member groups' own company shares. Such crossholding of shares has developed to prevent member companies being subject to a hostile takeover. Main members of the company groups gather at monthly meetings of the groups' presidents, called *shachokai*. Such meetings allow for important information concerning the groups to be shared and decisions to be discussed informally. This is quite a feat of organization when considering that these corporate groups can have more than 30 main companies and 200 subsidiary companies.

Cross-shareholding is diminishing in the horizontal groups largely because recent banking regulation does not allow latent gain from shares to raise the equity ratio. It has been the main reason why a cap was put on the amount of foreign share ownership, which usually amounted to less than a maximum of 5 per cent. With the decline of crossholdings, the 'poison pill' has emerged as a protection against hostile takeovers in mergers and acquisitions (M&A).[2]

Another pressure on the traditional crossholdings arrangement is current value accounting, which is being encouraged increasingly by the IASB and which may be causing a fall in profit when the re-evaluation of the cross-ownership shares occurs. Despite the Japanese GAAP, there is increasing pressure from the IASB and Japan's own need to become a fully-fledged member of the global economy that is making both the corporate governance system and the banking system more transparent and open to foreign investment. It is notable that Japan was initially reluctant to commit to the IASB through convergence. The Japan GAAP was a measure that looked to both the US GAAP and the IASB while adhering to the ASBJ. This has changed with the signing of the Tokyo Agreement and a new Project Plan based on the Agreement, which was published on 6 December 2007, outlining the steps towards achieving convergence with the IASB. The Keidanren, the Japanese employers' organization, and the top representatives of the four major auditing firms in Japan have been all positive towards the Tokyo Agreement.

Sir David Tweedie, Chairman of the IASB, pointed out on 25 December 2007 that, as shown by the timeline of the Tokyo Agreement, Japanese accounting standards are moving in the same direction as global standards and, importantly, there is now an expectation that Japan will participate fully in the development of global accounting standards. He noted further that Japan's participation, such as with the IP highway, has encouraged the USA to actually set a date to switch to International Financial Reporting Standards (IFRS). With Japan now supporting the IASB and China, India and Korea moving in the direction of meeting international standards, Japan is keen to be involved in setting the standards. This was confirmed in the joint ASBJ and IASB meeting held in Tokyo on 8 and 9 April 2008, and progress towards convergence according to the project plan was proceeding to plan.[3]

Essential changes to the Commercial and Company Codes

Company law in Japan has been a target of great reform under the Koizumi government's stewardship. Since 2002, the Working Group on Company Law of the Legislative Council, which is the consultative body of the Ministry of Justice, has led a drastic reform of company law, which also includes Part 2 of the Commercial Code, the Limited Liability Company Law and the Law of Exceptional Provisions to the Commercial Code Concerning the Audit of Stock Companies. The Working Group published the results of their deliberations in February 2005 and they were submitted to the Diet for approval. With a few amendments, which will be looked at where appropriate below, the reforms were approved by the Diet on 29 June 2005.

The basic reforms that have taken place under the Koizumi government include:

- securing the realization of corporate governance;
- bringing the law into line with the internationalization of corporate activity;
- modernizing terms and consolidating company law;
- bringing the law into line with the highly developed information society;
- improving fundraising measures.

One of the most fundamental tasks of the 2005 reform was similar to what occurred in the IP field, namely the modernization of the old language. So much of company, IP, economic and trade law has been archaic, preventing foreigners in particular from understanding its essence. Much of the frustration of foreign investors is not simply cultural and language difference but the extent to which the old language has been unintelligible and an impediment to doing business. In the case of the Commercial Code, until this reform it was written in the original language of the Meiji Era.

The current reformed company law, in accordance with the current social and economic situation, requires all companies to have at least a shareholders' meeting and a board of directors. Meanwhile, the structure of corporate governance, except for the shareholders' meeting and the board of directors, differs between a Company with Committees and a Company with a Corporate Auditor. The Exceptional Provisions provide different auditing system rules depending on the size of the company. The larger companies were not seen as a concern in relation to how close the shareholders are to the management, although how defence mechanisms are used and needed, especially when protecting an inefficient membership, is assessed among other reforms below. However, smaller closely held companies were a source of concern as the relationship between the management and shareholders is very close, which can bias decisions and may even open them to criminal elements. Therefore, the main target of the corporate governance reforms were concerned with the roles of shareholders and directors.[4]

New structure of corporate governance

Under the new law, all stock companies are required to have a shareholders' meeting and a director. In Articles 326–328 of the Company Code, a company may optionally set up bodies such as a board of directors, a corporate auditor or a board of corporate auditors, accounting consultant, an accounting auditor or the three committees of the nominating committee, audit committee and compensation committee.

In a company that has neither a corporate auditor nor committees, it is necessary to strengthen the shareholders' direct control. The new law provides the following rules.

First, part of the corporate auditors' power to audit execution is given to the shareholders. More specifically, shareholders are allowed to read the minutes of the board of directors without the permission of the court in a similar manner to corporate auditors (Article 371, para. 2, Company Code; cf. Article 371, para. 3, Company Code; Article 260-4, para. 6, Commercial Code). Shareholders have the right to demand convocation of meetings of the board of directors in cases of directors' malfeasance or conduct outside corporate purposes (Article 367, para. 1, Company Code; cf. Article 385, Company Code). Shareholders who demand convocation can attend the meeting of the board of directors and present their opinions (Article 367, para. 4, Company Code) as a corporate auditor can/must (Article 383, Company Code).

Second, the provision that permits a company to exempt a director from their liability through approval by a majority of directors or resolution of the board of directors (Article 426, Company Code) does not apply to these companies. This is the case because the exemption of a director's liability by a majority of directors or by resolution of the board of directors requires the approval of each corporate auditor or each member of the auditing committee (Article 426, para. 2, Company Code).

Third, in such companies where a director has discovered a fact that might be damaging to the company, it must be reported immediately to the shareholders' meeting, while a director of another type of company in a similar position must report the fact to a corporate auditor (Article 357, Company Code).

Finally, the requirements imposed on shareholders exercising their right to demand an injunction on directors' malfeasance in a company without a corporate auditor or committees (Article 360, para. 1, Company Code) are less strict than those in a Company with a Corporate Auditor or a Company with Committees (Article 360, para. 3, Company Code).[5]

The new Company Code as a reform measure

Although, by December 2006, the Japanese economy had experienced the most prolonged period of growth since the Second World War, the Japanese government and investors did not feel secure. This was despite the official discount rate having remained steady at 0.4 per cent since 14 July 2006 and the number of individual shareholders increasing every year for the previous decade. In fiscal year 2005, the number of individual shareholders increased from the previous year by 2,680,000 to 38,070,000.

In line with the thinking of the Koizumi government, greater flexibility for businesses to change their practices was enabled by the introduction of the Company Code on 1 May 2006. A number of key changes introduced by the new code include the following.

When a company appoints a director from outside the company at a shareholders' meeting, the reason for the appointment must be included in the reference documents for the general meeting to aid transparency of the internal procedures.

Traditionally, many companies held their shareholders' meetings on similar days in June so that *sokai-ya* (company racketeers) could not attend lots of shareholders' meetings, but the downside to this was that neither could individual small shareholders attend all the companies they had shares in. The Company Code adopted a provision from its predecessor, the Commercial Code, which allowed punishment of a person demanding that a company provide a benefit with the exercise of his/her right as a shareholder. The implementation of this has seen a decrease in the numbers of *sokai-ya* and less fear of intimidation by other shareholders. Holding shareholders' meetings on different days because of the new Company Code has led to an increase in attendance by individual shareholders who are also asking questions of management. Shareholders' meetings are increasing in length and there is a greater willingness to listen to shareholders, which impacts positively on share prices. Shareholders, in their turn, have very recently come to view the meetings as an opportunity to have direct communication with the company's management. Ordinary shareholders have shown a special interest in hostile takeovers and corporate scandals.

Another practice that the Company Code is altering is that of retirement remuneration, whereby the company is obligated by culture and tradition, not contract, to remunerate officers when they resign from the company. This practice is declining as companies adopt a performance-based remuneration system. Shareholders, especially foreign ones, do not understand the need for retirement remuneration. Under the Company Code, if the remuneration is fixed, the maximum amount of total remuneration must be decided at the shareholders' meeting or included in the articles of incorporation. If the remuneration is not fixed, the guidelines for the remuneration of directors must be decided at the shareholders' meeting, but if the remuneration is not pecuniary and comprises, for example, stock options, the plan must be decided in full at the shareholders' meeting.

Dividends form another area affected by the Company Code. Dividends in principle are fixed through resolutions made at shareholders' meetings, but may be made by the board of directors with certain provisos. These include the company having an accounting auditor, the term of office for directors not exceeding one year and the company being classified as a Company with a Corporate Auditor or a Company with Committees. The Company Code has added the condition that the company must put a provision in its articles of incorporation allowing the board of directors to fix the dividends.

The issue of whether shareholders or boards of directors should decide the fixing of dividends proved to be one of the most important issues to companies in fiscal year 2006. A low percentage of companies, less than a quarter, opted for boards of directors to fix dividends as most were conscious of the lack of approval from institutional investors and shareholders for such a scheme.

The Company Code also abolished the limitation on the frequency of distributing dividends, making the quarterly distribution of dividends possible. There is evidence that, as the Japanese economic upturn continues, so too will the distribution of dividends on a quarterly basis.

The Company Code appears to be widely accepted by Japanese business companies and has had a generally positive effect on internal corporate governance. What continues to be a worry for Japanese companies is external influence on corporate governance. The two main issues concern triangular mergers by foreign companies and defence measures against hostile takeovers, including the 'poison pill'.[6]

Triangular mergers by foreign companies

One of the essential points of the new Company Code, as mentioned above, is its flexibility, which makes it relatively easy for companies to reorganize. A central aspect of the code is how it has allowed for flexibility, if providing countervalue (*gappei taika*) for reorganization in terms of the assets that can be provided, which is applicable to mergers, reverse mergers by absorption and share exchanges.

According to the Company Code provision regarding M&A, which became effective on 1 May 2007, it is possible, when stock companies are merged, that shareholders of the dissolved companies may be issued shares of surviving stock companies as *gappei taika*. In addition, the code states that it is also permissible to provide *gappei taika* in the form of money or shares of the parent stock companies of the surviving companies. Mergers that use shares of the parent stock company to compensate shareholders of the absorbed company are called triangular mergers. This means that, in line with Japan's new willingness to globalize, foreign companies can merge Japanese stock companies with their subsidiaries incorporated in Japan. Therefore, in triangular mergers, the shareholder ratio of foreign stock companies with regard to their subsidiaries remains the same. Where the foreign stock companies engage in triangular mergers, in using their wholly owned subsidiaries as the surviving companies, the foreign stock companies continue to retain the successor stock companies as wholly owned subsidiaries.

The procedure for most mergers is similar to that carried out for triangular mergers, but in the latter it is essential to obtain approval from shareholders at their general meeting. In the case of Japanese stock companies being merged into subsidiaries of foreign stock companies, and where they are dissolved, the stock companies being dissolved must execute an agreement of merger with the subsidiaries that will be the surviving companies. It is also stipulated that the agreement must be approved at a general shareholders' meeting at least one day before the merger becomes effective. Yet, if the stock companies being dissolved are public stock companies and some or all of the *gappei taika* being given to their shareholders is restricted transfer shares or similar, the shareholders' approval requires passage of an extraordinary resolution. To increase flexibility, corporations are allowed to make these approvals subject to even stricter conditions by prescribing rules in their own articles and bylaws.

Resolutions of approval do not need to be obtained at shareholders' meetings for mergers whereby the surviving stock companies were already special controlling stock companies of the stock companies being dissolved. Shareholders' resolutions are necessary when some or all of the *gappei taika* being given is restricted – transfer shares and similar – and the stock companies being dissolved are public stock companies that do not issue different classes of shares. An example of not requiring approval at a general meeting of a Japanese stock company would be when a subsidiary stock company of a foreign stock company acquires over 90 per cent of all voting rights in a Japanese stock company and the foreign stock company then uses the subsidiary as the surviving stock company in a merger with the Japanese stock company.

Right of appraisal by shareholders

Shareholders of the stock companies that are being dissolved who are in opposition to the merger are allowed by the Company Code to demand that their stock companies buy back their shares at a fair price. In the case where a resolution at the shareholders' meeting is necessary to approve the merger, shareholders are compelled to take the following steps. They must first notify the stock company of their opposition prior to the shareholders' meeting being held. Second, they must vote against the merger at the shareholders' meeting. Once shareholders have taken these steps, they are allowed to demand that their shares be bought back by the company. The right of appraisal is granted as well to shareholders who cannot exercise their voting rights at shareholders' meetings and to shareholders in the case where a shareholders' resolution is not required for the merger.

Shareholders of Japanese stock companies that are being dissolved because of these appraisal rights can demand their shares be purchased by the stock companies, even when foreign stock companies and their subsidiaries are taking the initiative in triangular mergers.

Surviving stock companies

Surviving stock companies that are controlled by foreign stock companies will not have much difficulty in obtaining resolutions at their shareholders' meetings, when compared with the stock companies being dissolved.

In the case of triangular mergers, surviving stock companies transfer shares of their parent stock companies to shareholders of terminating stock companies. This means that surviving stock companies need to acquire and hold shares of their parent stock companies. According to the Company Act, subsidiary stock companies are prohibited from acquiring shares of parent stock companies. In the case of triangular mergers, subsidiaries are allowed to acquire shares of parent stock companies and hold the shares until the day when the merger becomes effective. In these circumstances, the total number of shares that subsidiaries are allowed to acquire must not exceed the number of shares they intend to provide to shareholders of the stock companies being dissolved.[7]

Triangular mergers and foreign companies

In 2007, the ruling LDP committee on legal affairs was concerned that foreign stock companies would use provisions of the Company Code concerning enhanced flexibility of using *gappei taika* to take over Japanese stock companies through such means as triangular mergers. However, the ordinance released on 13 March 2007 did not add amendments requiring shareholders' resolutions regarding triangular mergers by foreign stock companies to be held to stricter standards than ordinary resolutions. Consequently, such triangular mergers will not be considered an exception to the ordinary standards regarding the passage of resolutions at shareholders' meetings. The Nippon Keidanren were in the forefront in advocating the introduction of laws permitting triangular mergers in Japan. It did argue, however, that, under certain conditions in which the triangular mergers were carried out by foreign stock companies, the shareholders' resolutions approving such mergers should be held to a higher standard than ordinary resolutions. Yet, after taking into consideration that a contract must be concluded in advance between the surviving and dissolved stock companies agreeing to the merger and that the stock companies from either side must obtain resolutions consenting to the agreement of their own shareholders' meetings, it would generally be difficult to consider triangular mergers a type of hostile takeover.

Hostile takeovers

With the rise of triangular mergers giving foreign companies the ability to take over and dissolve Japanese companies and the decline in cross-shareholding as a defence mechanism, by 2006 a number of alternative defence measures were being adopted by Japanese companies. These defence measures afforded them protection from encroaching globalization and the flexibility of the new Company Code.

Some of the defence measures adopted and utilized at this time included cross-shareholding but on a lesser scale, stock acquisition rights, rights plans for trust banks, prior warning plans, stricter conditions on removing directors, a decrease in the number of directors, and a rise in authorized capital. It is also possible for companies to adopt a golden shares countermeasure but this option is not often used. Market mechanisms keep the defence measures from becoming irrational because, if such measures are prejudicial to the shareholders, the stock market will react and the stock market price of the company will fall. A well-known thwarting of an attempted hostile takeover through a 'white knight' approach occurred. This was the case of the Oji Paper Company, which attempted to acquire stock in the Hokuetsu Paper Company. The takeover was unsuccessful because of the timely intervention of a rival paper company, Nihon Paper. The most common defence measure is now becoming the 'poison pill', which is bringing with it a whole host of problems.[8]

The advent of the 'poison pill'

Traditionally, as shown in Chapter 2, Japanese social culture avoids direct confrontation and engages in hostile takeovers with the greatest reluctance. As cross-shareholding was the main defence mechanism against hostile takeovers, its decline has heralded serious debate regarding the rise of such takeovers and the 'poison pill' approach. During the Koizumi period, Japan found itself in a dilemma in that cross-shareholding, which keeps all corporate governance internal to Japanese companies against the rest of the world, could not be sustained with a policy of seeking foreign investment. Not to seek foreign investment meant the further demise of the Japanese economy, which desperately required injections of foreign capital to grow through the process of globalization. This openness to foreign investment also meant that defence measures utilized by economies of the West needed to be adopted. As shown in Chapter 3, concerning the law the Japanese will borrow processes from foreign countries as long as they leave the essence of the Japanese way of doing things intact.

The 'poison pill' approach falls within the Japanese Commercial Code of stock acquisition rights (*shinkabu-yoyakuken*), which refers to the rights under which the person who holds such rights makes a move against the company in order to obligate the latter to issue new shares to the rights holder. In the case of rights holders exercising this right, they must pay into the company an amount of money agreed beforehand for a specified period of time. This is known as a 'call option' within corporate finance.

The use of a stock acquisition right involves the following components. The first is a company giving the right to its directors and officers as a stock option. Second, in a venture company, a company gives the right to its directors and officers as a supplement in terms of compensation in cash. Third, a company uses it as a defence against takeover.

Two types of 'poison pill' in Japan

The 'poison pill' belongs to the final option and there are two paths that such a method may follow. The first type of 'poison pill' is the one used in the USA – the flip in/flip over 'poison pill'. This type entails the company issuing stock acquisition rights for free to all shareholders who hold common shares pro rata to the number of shares owned by the shareholders. Such a stock acquisition right can be exercised only when the bidder acquires more than a fixed rate of shares and the company can issue new shares to shareholders other than the bidder. Even in the case where the bidder acquires many shares, new shares are immediately issued by exercising the stock acquisition right in order to make a dilution of the bidders' shareholdings occur. This type of stock acquisition right can be redeemed by a resolution of the board of directors when it is not as yet exercised. Therefore, it creates incentives to the bidder to negotiate with the board of directors of the issuing company in order to have the 'pill' redeemed, so the board of directors is enabled to contain a destructive hostile takeover.

The other type of 'poison pill' process uses trusts. The company first issues the stock acquisition rights to a special purpose company (SPC), which is pursuant to a special resolution of the shareholders' meeting, and the SPC entrusts the stock acquisition rights to a trust bank. The beneficiaries of the trust are all shareholders other than the bidder and its related parties. The beneficiary rights can be exercised separately by the beneficiaries or collectively by the trust administrator. The stock acquisition rights may be exercised in the case of the occurrence of a certain trigger event. This could be when the bidder acquires more than the fixed rate of shares, giving beneficiaries the opportunity to request the issuance of new shares.

Another possibility exists whereby the company issues to a third party the class shares with veto rights on certain important business matters. This type of 'poison pill' is called the 'vaccine plan' in Japan. The difference to the two 'poison pills' above is the allocation of stock acquisition rights. In the US type, the stock acquisition rights are allocated to all shareholders who hold common shares. The second SPC type is allocated to a third party (although the issuing company has a friendly relationship with the third party) and the issuing company issues the class share, not the stock acquisition right.

Problems with the Japanese 'poison pill'

In the US type, it is quite difficult to decide whether the conditions surrounding the stock acquisition rights, in which the bidder cannot exercise such a right even if the bidder holds the right, traditionally violate the principle of equal treatment of shareholders. If such a principle is broken it would make the 'poison pill' approach invalid. This principle could be broken in the SPC type as well through disclosure in securities law and the cost by distributing the trust property among many shareholders.

The third-party solution also contains problems, because such outsiders acquire 'super powers' of the issuing company, so the management in the issuing company might prefer such outsiders' interest to that of general shareholders. This situation might have an adverse effect on corporate governance. Second, if such class shareholders unite with the bidder, the deterrent effects of a 'poison pill' will disappear. Third, if the company issues such class shares to directors and officers in the issuing company, it seems likely that this issue of class shares becomes more based on the self-interest of directors and officers.

Supporters of the 'poison pill' approach serve to stop companies from being ready targets for takeover bids, which are both costly and potentially damaging to the companies' reputations. They are costly because takeover bids usually give the impression that a company has management inefficiencies, so concerned customers and suppliers must be placated often with lower prices and other concessions. Headhunters are poised to steal the best employees, so expensive bonuses and incentives are often given. Company projects and major capital expenditure may be forced to be put on hold and creditors may delay commitments. Employees may also become discouraged from investing in the firm and their loyalty may weaken, as efforts may be wasted in the event a hostile takeover is successful. Although Japan has never experienced the very destructive takeovers that have occurred in the USA, many Japanese feel it is necessary to be prepared for such an eventuality.

'Poison pill' distrusted by foreigners

Foreigners who seek to engage in an M&A, hostile or otherwise, are concerned that a defence measure such as the 'poison pill' may not, in fact, be a mechanism to cover up the deficiencies of management, the latter wishing to entrench itself. It may appear that internal corporate governance that is far from satisfactory uses an external corporate governance mechanism for the purpose of self-preservation. It is possible that the bidder can plant a proxy fight to remove and replace the board of directors that refuses to redeem the pill and may negotiate with the board of directors to eliminate the pill. However, this would also mean that the 'poison pill' can only be stopped in the short term, but that this will not be effective in the long term. Yet, to enter into such a procedure is timely and costly as all proceedings would require monitoring by independent directors, courts and shareholders to be effective. However, the requirements for independent directors in Japan, according to the most recent Commercial Code, are more ambiguous than in the USA. The market in Japan is not as efficient as in the USA, so it cannot be assured that independent directors in Japan are truly independent of the companies that they are to monitor. The courts, therefore, would be the most independent of monitors, except that the Commercial Code amendments about stock acquisition rights are technical rather than substantive, which means that the court has no legislative guidelines about the 'poison pill'. This would leave foreign companies at a disadvantage if they chose to pursue the path of taking on the 'poison pill' defence measure.[9]

7 Future developments in the Japanese exchanges

Background

Although attempts to reform the Japanese securities exchange pre-date the Koizumi government and, as noted in Chapter 3, first occurred at the exchange's inception in the late nineteenth century, former Prime Minister Koizumi and his administration had a passion for structural reform that has surpassed that of any Japanese politician in recent history, and this provided much-needed impetus to make the economy and the TSE globally competitive. Dr Takenaka Heizo, whom Prime Minister Koizumi chose to be Minister of State for Economic and Fiscal Policy (see Chapter 1), notes in his book[1] the many ways the two worked together effectively to pave the way for essential economic reform: through eliminating unnecessary large-scale projects that only served the purpose of gaining rural votes; privatizing public corporations; reducing the issuance of national bonds; separating the vast private savings accounts from the Post Office to inject more of the savings into consumption to benefit the wider economy; and freeing the economy from the stranglehold of unwieldy, bureaucratic government, which had caused economic stagnation.

Part of the latter was connected to deregulation, which was a necessity in order for the TSE to be globally competitive. The other part was to upgrade the IT used by the TSE, so that it could operate on a global stage. The TSE lacked the modern technical mechanisms to make it able to cope with American or European technical advantages and turned to American technical know-how to upgrade its trading systems. However, what the TSE lacked, as did the other Japanese exchanges, was a viable market for the increasingly important SME sector, where much of the innovation that Japan needs so badly takes place.

Fears of the Japanese exchanges falling behind

Underlying the urgent activity of the TSE and other exchanges in Japan is a fear that, although Japan has the second largest stock market after New York and still constitutes the largest financial centre in Asia, it may be falling behind. More dynamic markets in Hong Kong, Singapore and, increasingly, Shanghai's Pudong are surging ahead in market capitalization. In 1990, Japan comprised a third of global market capitalization, while today that is less than one-tenth. This is troubling – as Japan strives to become more competitive through product innovation and the IP drives, it must also look to value-added financial services for greater growth. The TSE is attempting to reverse its fortunes through all the changes discussed below.

The most obvious concern for the TSE has been the decline in foreign listings from 125 in 1990 to 25 today, compared to 446 foreign listings in New York, 315 in London and 150 in the tiny city state of Singapore. As mentioned above, and as Takenaka Heizo stressed when a member of the Koizumi cabinet, upgraded IT systems are essential for TSE success. When the TSE IT system crashed because of a flood of orders a few years ago, it damaged the TSE's competitiveness. As seen in Chapters 1 and 4, the fact that Japanese accounting standards are moving towards unification with the IASB is essential for the TSE and other Japanese exchanges to prosper. Investors were becoming increasingly put off by the Japan GAAP, making it more difficult and costly to meet Japanese standards, which differed from international ones. The Japanese language is another barrier to foreign investors, but this is being addressed by allowing forms to be filled in English and relevant information to be available in the English language.

Another problem is the dearth of those who wish to take risk. The Japanese are traditionally risk-averse so many innovative financial products are waiting for investors. This is another reason why foreign investment, especially from foreign institutions, is being welcomed and sought to provide a lead on risk-taking. Yet, many foreign investors are put off because of the lack of financial products on offer, which in turn are so oversubscribed by a surplus of domestic funds that spreads and produces low yields that are not attractive to foreign investors. Deregulation of the TSE only occurred in 2001 and government bonds still dominate. As historical analysis showed in Chapter 3, the Japanese government has always tried to control industry, even private enterprise, to a certain extent. Government institutions that should assist private enterprise are intrusive, such as the FSA, which is more likely to investigate those who come to them with a problem than to understand the problem.

Reform in the securities exchanges and the SME sector

Dynamic growth in Europe and especially the UK derives from the SME sector, which is creating thousands of new companies that wish to list on bespoke exchanges that cater to their particular financial requirements.[2] The problem has been that nothing exists in Japan that accommodates the smaller companies and spin-outs that are the drivers of innovation in Europe. The mechanisms have been created to produce innovative spin-outs, such as the TLOs at universities, and organizations such as AIST (see Chapter 2)[3] that consolidate ideas in incubation and commercialize them, but there is no existing mechanism or market such as AIM (Alternative Investment Market – the LSE's international market for smaller growing companies) through which these companies can list and grow.

Mothers (market of the high-growth and emerging stocks), the alternative type of market of the TSE, should accommodate such small companies and innovative spin-outs but will not accept companies under a certain size and, given its structure and the past problems and obstacles presented to small companies listing, the only alternative is an adjunct or completely new exchange that caters for Japanese SMEs no matter how small. This can only be done by drawing in and on the institutions in Japan that deal with and sustain SMEs. The institutions that sustain SMEs in Japan range from the government, universities and businesses, to banking and insurance groups. There is an attempt to create a new feeder mechanism that channels the most appropriate companies into a new growth market that caters to their needs and that the large financial institutions have no interest in blocking.

The LSE has successfully created a market – AIM – that caters to such innovative companies that are both wealth-creating and dynamic. Mr Saito Atsushi, President and CEO of the TSE, states that he believes that the successes of the LSE AIM can be replicated in Japan:

> Last October, the Tokyo Stock Exchange announced our intentions to jointly build a new market in Japan for professionals with the London Stock Exchange that targets emerging companies both domestic and abroad, particularly those located in Asia.
>
> I am confident that an enhanced Japanese capital market backed by an enormous amount of Japanese financial assets will bring about a more effective redistribution of risk money throughout the Asian region and to other parts of the world.[4]

Japan, contrary to popular belief, is not just an economy based on the massive *sogo shosha/keiretsu*, but has many SME companies and, since the Koizumi government with its emphasis on innovation, added value and intellectual property rights, has encouraged a dynamic innovative sector that is serving to turn around a decade of economic stagnation. Mothers has been the market for SMEs listing in Japan. However, the TSE has realized that Mothers has been geared towards companies that are not strictly SMEs in size, according to market capitalization at the time of IPO (initial public offering), amount of funds raised or current profits (see Figure 7.1).

The TSE is in the process of making its markets more globally competitive and less inward looking and is committed to enhancing investors' confidence in the market, while promoting a balance between the often vigorous corporate action of listed companies and the necessary protection required for investors. The TSE is also committed to supporting greater transparency. To understand the development of the Japanese exchanges it is important to understand the future plans to create an AIM-like exchange in Japan for dynamic SMEs to list successfully and the recent changes and plans to improve the listing system on the TSE's Mothers.

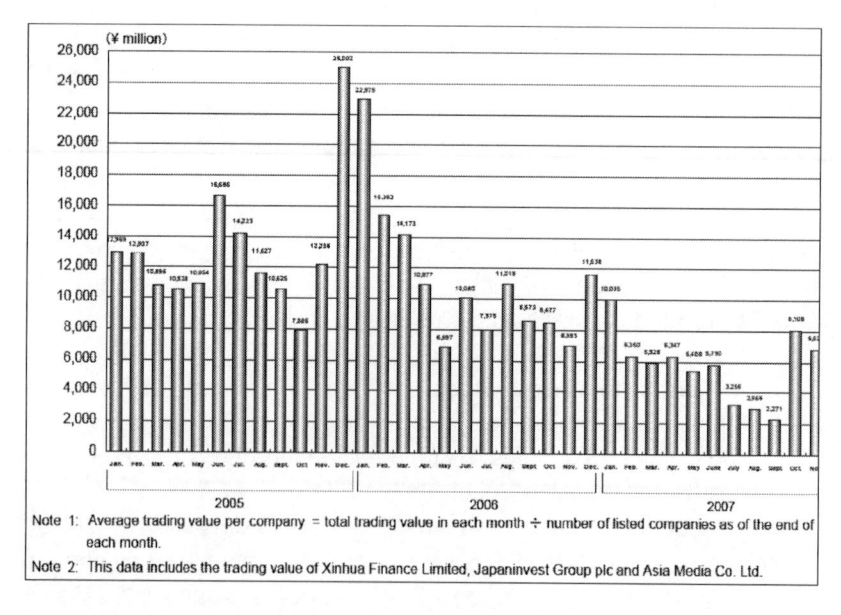

Figure 7.1 Average trading value per company.[5]

Plans for a new AIM-like market

The basic problem for SMEs in Japan is in terms of listing possibilities. The LSE and TSE intend to rectify this situation by working together and transferring some of the success of AIM to the Japanese markets to make them more globally competitive through structural reform in the following manner.

- AIM, according to the LSE, is one of the most successful growth markets in the world today, and its success as a market has been caused by its companies attracting long-term institutional investment; institutional investors now hold £55 billion of the market, up £12 billion on 2006. Further issues account for over 40 per cent of the £52.6 billion raised by AIM companies to date – a testament to the quality of the companies on the market.
- It is clear from talking to market participants that there is a funding gap currently in existence in Japan for SMEs looking to gain access to early-stage risk capital. The LSE has tested its philosophy regarding exporting knowledge from its experience with AIM with market participants who are keen to work with the TSE and LSE to take this forward. According to the LSE, people are impressed with the collective vision that the LSE and the TSE share. They have both made good progress with their goal of finding a set of competent potential nomads and specialists so that the key stakeholders understand their plans. They are all keen to be involved in building a community that will support the new market and companies seeking to raise finance through this new route to market. In the last year, AIM generated over £1 billion in revenues for advisers, which has been a key driver in economic growth in the UK. The LSE therefore expects there to be a similar accelerator effect in the Japanese economy when the new market is launched. According to the LSE, AIM in the UK has been so successful because the relationship between advisers and AIM companies has been, and continues to be, mutually beneficial and has delivered real economic and business value for the participants involved.
- The main candidates for the new market will be SMEs and emerging companies that are confronting a funding gap in the current market, and that had historically relied upon personal and bank loans, or that are not yet sufficiently developed for other public markets. The exchanges expect the initial candidates to be emerging Japanese companies that are at the growth stage, but that are perhaps not yet sufficiently established to be listed on Mothers (see Figure 7.1 above and text below). It is both exchanges' view that the introduction of the

new market will fill a significant gap and will stimulate venture capital investment and other investment in SMEs and emerging companies in Japan by providing another possible exit route, which has simply not existed in the past in Japan for venture capital firms or entrepreneurs looking to grow their businesses. AIM has developed a distinct identity in the UK and there now exists a community of AIM companies that are benefiting from being on the world's most arguably successful SME market. Other fast-growing companies aspire to a flotation on AIM as, according to the LSE, it can deliver real economic value to their businesses. It can also act as a stamp of approval for their businesses and deliver a profile that they can leverage in their business relationships (i.e. with suppliers and peers). The LSE expects the new market to deliver these same benefits, listed above, for Japanese companies.

- The experience with AIM proves to the LSE that it is possible to create a market structure that attracts quality smaller companies and allows them to gain capital early in their growth cycle, providing investors with exposure to some exciting companies at the steepest part of their growth curve. The LSE expects that this will be an attractive opportunity for international investors from around the region. In common with institutional investors globally, Japanese institutions are increasingly aware of the need to diversify their holdings, which is something that this market can help them to achieve. Educating investors about the new market will be an important part of its development, and this is something that the TSE, the LSE and the advisory community involved with the new market will make a priority.
- The new market will be a clearly delineated risk capital-based market, and as such it is likely to be attractive to companies that are not as well established as those on Mothers. These companies may not yet be ready to meet with Mothers' specific requirements, which are more geared to the requirements of Japanese retail investors. The LSE and the TSE are discussing the details of this, but, for example, they anticipate that the new market may be excluded from the J-SOX (Japan's Financial Instruments and Exchange Law) rules and may not demand quarterly financial reporting, in the Japanese GAAP (see Chapter 1) and in the Japanese language.[6]

Programme for improving the listing system for the TSE and Mothers

The TSE Mothers is concerned with being globally competitive and increasing investors' confidence in the market and has embarked on a programme to make the listing system more transparent and user friendly. This is being done through a number of measures to improve the listing system for the future and is at various stages of completion.

Basic practical policies are to be addressed, including:

- While corporations carry out their activities freely, in the cases where this involves the hindrance of timely disclosure of information, impairs the certainty of stock price formation and leads to unfair transactions, the TSE will be proactively involved in such cases.
- There will be improvements in the criteria for the listing examination, more in-depth descriptions of the items to be disclosed, confirmation of the system to improve disclosures after listing, the grouping of stock issues in their attributes and the issuance of warnings from the viewpoint of protecting investors.
- While the rules for exit from the market may relate solely to non-compliance with fundamental duties as listed companies except in the cases of bankruptcy, insufficient liquidity or very low market capitalization, the effects of the exit rules on the market are so great that the TSE is considering extending the types of enforcement action available.
- In the case of foreign listed companies that are primarily traded on the TSE market, various measures corresponding to their forms and operations will be taken, while respecting the market policies or legal systems of their home countries.

Actual implementation to date of improvements in listing

The TSE Mothers is raising awareness of listed companies and creating an environment in which investors can more easily use corporate information. Part of this improvement is greater disclosure of information on MSCBs (moving strike convertible bonds), for example, and capital increases through the allotment of shares to third parties.

The adoption of the quarterly report system under J-SOX (including the integration of the semi-annual report system into the quarterly report system, which became effective in April 2008) means that the TSE will take necessary measures, such as the integration of the interim earnings digest system and the quarterly financial and performance disclosure system.

The TSE is making preparations for providing account settlement information in the form of XBRL, which is an accounting tool to promote sophisticated use of financial settlement data through the renovation of the Timely Disclosure Network.

On 1 November 2007, the TSE amended its relevant listing rules to include a requirement that listed companies take appropriate corporate activity measures for the purpose of the protection of shareholders and investors and proper market operation. (See the TSE Corporate Code of Conduct with reference to corporate activities). Some of the changes will include:

- Improvements in the exercise of voting rights at general shareholders' meetings will involve the diversification of the dates of general shareholders' meetings; early mailing and distribution of convocation notices and their posting on the websites; and preparation of materials in English. The general rules for listed companies will now state that the listed company should respect the functions of the secondary markets and the rights of shareholders and investors. The Corporate Code of Conduct will include fundamental issues related to corporate governance to enhance the quality of companies listed on the market for emerging companies. Listed companies, therefore, other than large-scale companies defined in the Corporation Law, will also be required to decide establishment of the board of auditors (the audit committee), the accounting auditor system and the internal control system stipulated by the Corporation Law (the system to ensure appropriate business operation).
- Any listed company with fewer than 1,000 shareholders will also be required to deliver shareholders' meeting reference documents (or any reference documents for the grant of proxy rights) to all of its shareholders.
- On 1 November 2007, the TSE prescribed methods to ensure the effectiveness of the items contained in the Corporate Code of Conduct in accordance with the compliance necessary and concreteness of acts and to implement phases of items in which companies may be delisted, items for public announcement and the imposition of requirements for voluntary measures by listed companies.
- The TSE will state clearly in its rules concerning 'corporate governance' and the 'effectiveness of the internal management system' as substantive listing examination items, in tandem with the development of the Corporate Code of Conduct, and will develop new examination criteria by integrating the essential parts of the listing examination into these areas.

- On 25 June 2007, the TSE made clear publicly its views on listing a company owned by a parent company in terms of it being inappropriate under the listing system to prohibit listing of a company owned by a parent company. However, given that there are issues that may give rise to adverse effects and issues that may result in conflicts of interest with minority shareholders, and given that listed companies have been required to substantially consolidate their management under the recent management environment, the listing of a company owned by a parent company may not necessarily be viewed as a desirable capital policy for many market players, including investors.
- The TSE and other Japanese exchanges announced to the public jointly that the TSE will discuss relevant issues with other exchanges to prevent the listing of a parent company and a subsidiary that are in fact managed as one company.
- In April 2008, the TSE were to announce to the public and amend the rules in relation to listed examination and listing supervision in connection with the internal control reporting system under J-SOX. Listed companies are required to have a relevant internal control system to ensure confidence in disclosure and any company that wishes to list its stock will also be required to improve the internal control after its listing.

Improvements to the listing systems, especially for Mothers

In relation to the Mothers market, the TSE has, since 1 November, amended its rules to improve the listing system so that the nature of Mothers can be more easily defined, and this will provide opportunities to gain earlier access to the capital market to companies that are in their initial stages of growth and intend to list their stocks in the First or Second Sections in the future.

The TSE has abolished the listing rules regarding reassignment from the First or Second Section market to Mothers. The TSE has also abolished current listing examination criteria related to sales and will not apply the delisting related to sales for five years from the time of the listing in order to promote the listing of companies with high growth potential.

The listing system has also been improved to enhance liquidity when companies are initially listed on Mothers. To alleviate liquidity shortage at the time of the initial listing of a company on Mothers, the TSE will review the listing examination criteria relating to share distribution and require a certain ration level for shares held by the special few at the initial listing of the company. As Mothers is a market for emerging companies with high growth potential, the TSE will determine an appropriate level of liquidity.

The TSE has, since May 2007, held seminars for the management of companies listed on Mothers to deepen the understanding of directors/officers of their responsibilities as managers of publicly traded companies.

Under discussion at present, with no plans for immediate implementation, is whether the TSE should ask Mothers-listed companies that fail to grow after a certain period to exit.

Further improvements to the TSE to make it globally competitive

The TSE will also consider innovations to assist public investors in fully understanding risks unique to investing in emerging companies with high growth potential.

The TSE will coordinate with related parties on the consolidation and unification of trading units. It will call for the cooperation of other exchanges in Japan to develop action plans. The TSE will continue to coordinate with related parties, such as listed companies, securities companies, transfer agents and JASDEC (Japan Securities Depository Center – a venture capital organization in Japan). The TSE has already begun discussion on trading units at the working group established for this purpose.

The TSE has requested listed companies for the consolidation of trading units. It announced to the public the 'Action Plan for the Consolidation of Trading Units' as a result of the discussion at the working group. Amendments to the relevant rules occurred in April 2008. What this means in real terms is that, as consensus is built, the TSE will develop and publicize action plans to realize unification to a trading unit of 100 shares as a basic lot in the future, and consolidation of the trading units to 100 shares and 1,000 shares as basic lots prior to the eventual unification. Setting a specific transitional period from the introduction of the dematerialization of stock certificates, the TSE will consolidate trading units per basic lot to those composed of 100 shares and 1,000 shares.

Additionally, revisions made to the listing rules to require accelerated application of the consolidated trading unit by newly listed companies, or companies planning to revise their basic lots or set new basic lots prior to completion of the consolidation, may be considered.

On 1 November 2007, relevant rules were amended with regard to the number of shareholders in the delisting criteria, so that the required number of shareholders will be fixed at a certain level instead of an increase being required. They were also amended in relation to the introduction of criteria for the number of floating shares and the market capitalization of such shares. When a company is initially listed or assigned to the First Section, the TSE will require the number and market capitalization of floating shares to exceed a specific number and value based on the formula determined by the TSE. If the number or market capitalization of floating shares of a company falls below specific criteria based on a formula determined by the TSE, the TSE will delist or reassign the stock of the company with such floating shares.

A review of the criteria for the shareholding ration of the special few was undertaken in the rules on 1 November 2007, with the TSE having revised its method of calculating the shareholding ration of the special few in light of the recent changes in shareholder structure. With the introduction of criteria for the number and market capitalization of floating shares, the TSE has revised the delisting criteria into those applied to companies whose number of floating shares is extremely fixed, as the shareholding ration of the special few exceeds 95 per cent. With regard to the listing examination criteria, the TSE has continued to call for the current level in order to ensure smooth transactions by alleviating high levels of price fluctuations immediately after listing. The TSE has also applied the criteria for the shareholding ration of the special few in terms of the examination of the listing on Mothers in accordance with the same purpose noted above. The TSE has applied for looser criteria for Mothers than for the First and Second Section markets, as Mothers is operated for emerging companies with high growth potential. A number of secondary implementations continue to be considered, including required amendments to the treatment of market segmentation in the case of initial listing on the First or Second Section and the treatment of market segmentation in the case of assignment from Mothers to the First or Second Section. In all these considerations, the TSE will take into account the continuity of TOPIX (Tokyo Stock Price Index) – widely accepted by investors and the Corporate Code of Conduct for companies listed on the First Section.

The TSE has made a structural adjustment to establish a market segment for problematic issues. It has improved its listing system to introduce a system in which the TSE will transfer a listed company to a market segment separate from the First and Second Sections and Mothers, to supervise it in cases where the TSE has found serious breaches in the listing rules by the listed company, which, however, does not fall under the delisting criteria and needs to request for redressing, or where the TSE has detected issues to improve through its confirmation of the internal management system of the listed company.

The TSE is continually improving transparency and fairness of decisions in the event that it takes disadvantageous measures against listed companies, such as a decision to delist. The TSE group established in the autumn of 2007 a self-regulatory corporation with reinforced independence. Fairness and transparency of decisions are improving as the self-regulatory corporation makes such decisions.

The TSE has reviewed the current name of the supervision post, while different names have been given separately for cases where the TSE is carrying out a delisting examination and for cases with other grounds. Thus, the TSE will introduce measures by which investors can easily understand that the TSE is carrying out a delisting examination.

By April 2008, the TSE, as a result of the findings of a working group, which made the suggestion in its report, established a period during which stocks that are in delisting post are flexible. On an ongoing basis, the TSE will consider providing a wide variety of instruments permitted to be listed on exchanges in the USA and Europe in response to investors' needs. It will call upon related parties to make necessary improvements not only in the listing system, but also in other systems, in order to list various instruments.

Future considerations

The TSE will discuss widely and consider approaches to revitalize the foreign stock market with a view to truly globalizing the TSE market. It will discuss and consider introducing more transparent procedures with respect to the performance of self-regulatory operations carried out by the self-regulatory corporation. In order to further enhance the transparency of listing examination operations and listing supervision, the TSE will continue to discuss and consider the implementation of various measures and policies, including clarification of basic ideas regarding decision-making.

To improve the system for preventing insider trading, the TSE is considering establishing an Insider Information Centre (this is a possible name for the centre) responsible for collecting and managing data on directors and officers of listed companies and making system improvements. The TSE will discuss and consider establishing the Insider Information Centre as a system for targeting all the listed companies on stock exchanges in Japan and granting all the securities companies with access to it. This is based on the premise that it will be established and operated by the TSE as a system with actual costs and expenses borne by the securities companies who are users. On the premise that full attention is directed to the handling of information on individuals, it is contemplated that the TSE will stipulate in the listing rules that listed companies register data (names, addresses and so forth) on their directors and officers within a specified scope with the Insider Information Centre in a timely and appropriate manner.[7]

Timely measures

It is possible to see from the above timely measures already taken, or to be implemented or still in the discussion stage, that the TSE has taken very seriously the possibility that they will fall behind other Asian exchanges while lagging even further behind New York, London and other European exchanges. The Koizumi administration sounded the clarion call for Japanese financial institutions to wake up to the reality of an increasingly globally competitive world that is fast outstripping Japan in the competitive stakes. The TSE has heeded this call, but whether the current administrations have the will or the mandate from their parties, or the ability to appeal directly to the populace and LDP party members, remains to be seen. These issues will be discussed in Chapter 8.

8 Conclusion

Lack of unification of direction

Since the resignation of Prime Minister Abe Shinzo after one disastrous year, and the appointment of Prime Minister Fukuda Yasuo and, subsequently, Aso Taro, a unified direction in terms of continuing economic structural reform, the IP drive and boosting foreign investors' confidence to promote globalization has waxed and waned. The unification of purpose that Japan required so desperately to pull itself out of the economic morass of the 1990s has become divided and weakened. Japanese people are once again losing trust and confidence in the economy and are not spending as freely as before. This and other events, to be described below, are giving foreign investors the jitters, which is having a knock-on effect throughout the economy. There are bright spots and continued support for a free market economy in the form of the new Governor of the BOJ, but different factions in Japan are now pulling in disparate directions. The last Prime Minister, Fukuda Yasuo, who was from the old school of politics, held steady but was unable to direct the turbulence into a more positive direction. Appealing directly to the populace did not seem to be Mr Fukuda's mode of operation, nor did 'swimming around' the entrenched bureaucrats and special interest groups. The performance of the new Prime Minister, Aso Taro, will be discussed later.

The pensions debacle

Many cynical Japanese began to use the *kanji* (Chinese characters) for deception to describe events in 2007. This was because Japanese stocks showed the worst performance of any large equity market, economic growth and performance were disappointing, domestic consumption and wages were stagnant, and house construction slowed because of stricter building earthquake codes being instituted during the summer of 2007. The final misery was the revelation under the Abe administration that 50 million pension records were lost. This occurred after the cautious optimism that was cultivated during the Koizumi years was abruptly brought to an end by the aforementioned events. The pension debacle has been steadily eroding trust in the government, as an ageing population are already concerned about their pensions.

Of the 50 million pensioners, 20 million are unable to be easily identified, while 10 million are seen to be nearly impossible to identify. To complicate matters, the onus is on the people to prove that the government is wrong, even though it is the government's record-keeping and squandering of pooled pensions that are at fault. During the bubble economy pensions were invested in resorts at which people were not interested in staying. Many resorts were part of the misuse of funds on white elephant projects that would buy the rural vote. Many Japanese people then became suspicious of the actual worth of their pensions and, on the whole, stopped paying in with impunity. Ironically, Prime Minister Fukuda was found in 2004 not to have paid his national pension premiums. Shortly after this revelation he resigned as Mr Koizumi's chief cabinet secretary. In addition, three other cabinet ministers, Nagagawa, Aso, the current Prime Minister, and Ishiba, had missed payments or had even failed to enter the pension scheme. Last year, it seemed to be a simple case of matching records, but now it was partially a case of lost records as well. Although it is not the case that people have lost their pensions completely, the loss of some entitlements has caused great anger among the predominantly ageing population.

The Japanese are a stoical people, but an issue as important as pension entitlement in an ageing population could not be more incendiary. What exacerbated the situation was Prime Minister Abe's lack of forthright disclosure, which has damaged and weakened the LDP until this day as, with every election issue, the public vents its anger upon the LDP. The 'solution' to the pension problem, which was represented by the government as political will over bureaucratic resistance, included (1) the abolition of the time limit for submission of claims for pensions; and (2) the establishment of a third-party committee to determine the legitimacy of benefit claims by participants unable to produce receipts for their payments. Whether these measures will see the end of the pension debacle with the trust of the populace restored remains to be seen.[1]

Worcestershire and Bull-Dog Sauces and the 'poison pill'

One continuing obstacle to foreign investment that is thwarting Japan's attempt to truly globalize is the 'poison pill' strategy discussed in

Chapter 6. In mid-July 2007, Japan's benchmark stock index was heading towards a seven-year high. The then Financial Services Minister, Yamamoto Yuji, made clear in ill-timed comments that a US fund's failure to buy a Japanese Worcestershire Sauce maker would have little or no impact on market confidence. Mr Yamamoto stated: 'It is impossible that the defeat of a foreign investment fund in only one court case would discourage overseas investors from participating in the Japanese stock market'. His remarks were quoted on the front pages of most prominent newspapers. The result in the following four months was a collapse that wiped out nearly £485 billion and the heaviest sellers were overseas investors. By comparison, the US sub-prime mortgage crisis has caused a mere loss of roughly £5.3 billion on Japanese banks. Added to this, the Tokyo stock market, because of its high liquidity and 28 per cent ownership by foreign investors, has served to absorb the troubles on Wall Street and in the City of London. Liquid investment from Tokyo has been taken to cover damage elsewhere.

Probably the most damaging outcome of all this turmoil is again with attempted sauce takeovers. Following Mr Yamamoto's speech, Steel Partners Japan Fund attempted to buy out the Bull-Dog Sauce Company, but it was thwarted by a very controversial 'poison pill' defence strategy. Many other Japanese companies – over 200 – have followed suit with the 'poison pill' defence, which has had a highly negative impact on the possibilities of further M&A activity moving forward.[2]

Although Japan has accepted the principle of M&A and the reality of hostile takeovers, it also believes in defensive measures, the 'poison pill', as mentioned in Chapter 6, being a primary and developing strategy. The majority of foreign companies are not enamoured of the 'poison pill' and see it as a measure to protect inefficient Japanese management and vested interests. The Bull-Dog Sauce Company case is a prime example of the continuing problem between what Japanese companies consider to be acceptable and a largely different Western perception that will continue to cause problems for the future of the Japanese economy unless there is some sort of resolution. In this final chapter we assess the Bull-Dog Sauce case to highlight some of the more important underlying causes at stake that will affect globalization plans by the Japanese for their economy.

By the end of July 2007, 381 listed companies had adopted some type of defensive measure against hostile takeover and 353 of these companies, or 92.7 per cent, sought approval for defensive measures at shareholders' meetings. Although, in principle, defensive measures to protect management itself should not be allowed, a major question that has been troubling overseas investors is whether a specific shareholder, who is a hostile takeover bidder, should be allowed to be treated by management differently from other shareholders. The Bull-Dog Sauce case, which followed a US fund's failure to buy a Japanese Worcestershire Sauce maker, has made Western companies cautious at best and unwilling at worst to engage in M&A activity in Japan, and this is harming Japan's attempts to globalize its economy.

Unequal treatment of shareholders?

In the Bull-Dog Sauce case, there was concern that shareholders were being treated unequally, namely the American shareholders, Steel Partners, who are an investment fund. On 18 May 2007, Steel Partners made a public announcement that it would begin a takeover bid to acquire the remaining outstanding shares of Bull-Dog Sauce. This takeover bid was then submitted to the head of the Kanto Local Finance Bureau on the same day. In the beginning, the purchasing period of the takeover bid was from 18 May until 28 June and the price offered per share was 1,584 yen. Yet, on 15 June the purchasing period was extended to 10 August and the price increased to 1,700 yen per share. The initial share offer added a premium of between 12.56 and 12.82 per cent, which Steel Partners believed to be appropriate for the market price. On 25 May, Bull-Dog Sauce submitted to the head of the Kanto Local Finance Bureau a report with detailed questions concerning Steel Partners' takeover bid.

The report detailing the answers, and which gave rise to concerns on the part of the majority of Bull-Dog shareholders, stated that Steel Partners had no experience of managing companies in Japan and had no plans to do so; that Steel Partners had no intention of managing Bull-Dog directly; that Steel Partners could not show its management proposals for enhancing the value of Bull-Dog Sauce; and that Steel Partners had no intention of managing the daily operations of Bull-Dog Sauce.

On 7 June, the board of Bull-Dog Sauce made a decision to oppose the takeover bid and, on the same day, proposed a shareholders' meeting on 24 June. At this meeting, a number of defensive measures were put forward to the shareholders. The first proposal was that the articles of incorporation be changed so that extraordinary approval by shareholders would be required for any matter concerning allotting rights to purchase new shares without consideration. The second proposal was that, if the Proposal to Change the Articles was approved, an allotment of rights to purchase new shares be enacted. According to the Proposal to Change the

Articles, Bull-Dog Sauce would make a decision concerning allotting rights to purchase new shares, including treating certain shareholders differently from other shareholders in terms of acquiring and exercising the rights. The decision by Bull-Dog Sauce was made through its board of directors and also through the approval of the shareholders' meeting, with approval of the latter being required to be very high. At the actual meeting on 24 June, both the Proposal to Change the Articles and the Proposal of Allotment were approved by 88.7 per cent and 83.4 per cent, respectively, of attending shareholders' total voting rights. Following this approval, the Bull-Dog Sauce board of directors adopted an outline of the Allotment of Rights without Consideration. After confirming the matter to the Tax Agency, the board of directors made the decision to acquire all the rights that Steel Partners' Associates held at the rate of 396 yen per right, without imposing any burdens or duties on Steel Partners' Associates.

The court decision

On 13 June, before the shareholders' meeting, Steel Partners filed an action for a provisional decision to suspend the Allotment of Rights without Consideration, making the claim that Article 247 of the Company Code would be applied directly or using analogous interpretation. Steel Partners argued that the Allotment of Rights without Consideration would contravene the principle of equality of shareholders, the laws and regulations and the articles of incorporation and was grossly unfair.

The court of first instance agreed that Article 247 of the Code would apply in relation to the principle of equality of shareholders. Yet, the court also stated that the Allotment of Rights without Consideration would not be against the intended meaning of the principle of equality, did not contravene the relevant laws and would not be grossly unfair. The application for an injunction was dismissed by the court.

Steel Partners then appealed, but the court of appeal held that, considering that the Allotment of Rights without Consideration was necessary, reasonable and a rational measure to prevent detriment to the corporate value of Bull-Dog Sauce, and that Steel Partners' Associates was a so-called 'abusive takeover bidder', the Allotment of Rights without Consideration would not be against the principle of equality of shareholders, nor would it contravene the law or be grossly unfair. Steel Partners then appealed to the Supreme Court, but its appeal application was dismissed.[3]

A case of shifting goalposts

The Bull-Dog Sauce case has been seen by some Western observers as a case of shifting goalposts to block out foreign investors when it suits Japanese companies. However, in this particular case, the hostile takeover bidder, Steel Partners, was found to have no management experience of companies in Japan and not to have any plans to enhance the value of the target company. It was a company trying to stop itself from being asset-stripped and destroyed in the eyes of the shareholders, and was not simply a case of trying to protect an incompetent management, which should not be allowed. Defence measures that are rational should be allowed, but it is becoming a difficult area in which to define terms, because there is a growing tendency in all cases of foreign investors trying to take over Japanese companies to treat hostile takeover bidders and normal shareholders differently. The real danger is that the tendency is for Japan Incorporated to reconstitute itself in a new form, shutting out the very foreign investment that it needs for a long-term recovery, eschewing any real form of globalization in the final result.

Using the 'poison pill' may eventually poison the economic recovery Japan so desperately needs, especially with Asian competitors nipping at its heels. The dilemma Japan is facing economically can be seen clearly in the stalemated political situation.

Political deadlock in the Diet

After experiencing a very decisive administration in the form of the Koizumi government, Japan had a deadlock in the Diet under Prime Minister Fukuda, who served as chief cabinet secretary in the Koizumi administration, and was known to have said frequently, 'There is no point in telling Prime Minister Koizumi. He will not listen.' Perhaps there is a message here, given the current state of affairs in the Diet, that someone needs to be in charge, making informed decisions rather than constantly bowing to divisive factionalism.

Prime Minister Fukuda, who has always shown competency, was finding it especially difficult to have his policies pushed through the Diet, as the two houses were led by two different parties. Fukuda tried very hard to reconcile differences through his cabinet reshuffle, which notably made Aso Taro General Secretary of the party. This was a key post and a bold move as it gave Fukuda's former rival in the previous year's election increasing power while unifying the LDP. Unfortunately, with only one year until September 2009, when a general election has to be called to re-elect the House of Representatives, the emphasis shifted from policies to which party would win the next election. While the Fukuda administration attempted to resolve issues such as rising prices, the pension crisis, reform of the tax system and the Indian Ocean refuelling law, which was due for renewal in January 2009, the LDP General Secretary Aso Taro and the Democratic Party of Japan (DPJ), led by Ozawa Ichiro – known previously as a former 'Young Turk' because of his historic association with Mr Koizumi, challenged Mr Fukuda's policies and *raison d'être*. In terms of economic policy, Mr Fukuda thought he was making headway in reconciling those in his party who believed the way forward was to raise taxes and cut the huge budget deficit through curtailing government spending, and the financial conservatives who believed the hated consumption tax should be raised to deal with the remaining deficit after cutting government expenditure.

Resignation of Fukuda and election of Aso

Fukuda's attempts to minimize conflict in the Diet became futile during his struggles in June, July and August 2008. In July, Aso Taro began to put forward the idea that the government should postpone its target to eliminate deficit in the primary balance, which is the general current account balance that excludes debt service and new borrowing, by 2011. This threw any agreement achieved by the Fukuda administration into disarray. Added to this pressure, Ozawa tried to force the Fukuda cabinet to step down. The DPJ proposed a 2.7 trillion yen emergency fiscal stimulus package in July 2008 to deal with the sharp rise in crude oil prices, which was largely a package designed to appeal to potential voters in the next general election. The huge spending cuts proposed, coupled with achieving equilibrium in the primary balance and postponing the 2011 target, would have given the Fukuda government more breathing space, but would also have destroyed the reform measures instituted under the Koizumi administration.

By 1 September, Mr Fukuda announced his resignation, in order to prevent another Diet session where nothing would be accomplished because of all the blocks by the opposition parties and the DPJ in particular. On 22 September 2008, the LDP held an election, with the front runner, Aso Taro, who favours fiscal stimulus, being elected on 24 September as the new Prime Minister of Japan.

Japan showing the way forward?

The new Governor of the BOJ, who took office on 9 April 2008 after wrangling in the Diet caused a vacuum in the post for three weeks, calmed the money markets and also made Japan a source of liquidity to draw on for ailing sectors in the American and European markets. Uncertainty in the top banking post in the world's second largest economy had not been helpful to world market performance.[4]

The falling value of the yen vis-à-vis the weakening dollar has been seen by some as an opportunity for the Japanese to actually profit from global financial ills through the great pools of liquid cash that Japan holds. Tamura Kotaro, a Japanese lawmaker, even suggested that Japan could save the world financial markets through its enormous savings, including $US 950 billion in foreign reserves and $US 1.5 trillion in pension funds, as well as the $US 15 trillion in personal financial assets of its people. The Japanese people are very risk averse and have a tendency towards saving, even when the interest rate is as low as the current 0.5 per cent. In 2007, before the global financial troubles sparked by sub-prime lending in the USA, many Japanese people, including housewives, felt confident enough to buy shares in companies in China and elsewhere on the internet. Now, this activity has dried up and the Japanese are saving with a vengeance, especially in light of the pension debacle, which is continuing to blight the current government under Aso Taro. A few months ago an enraged pensioner, who had his pension details lost by the government, stabbed and killed a retired minister who had worked in the pension division of the government. Japanese people are raised to be restrained and to cooperate, so this is an example of the strength of feeling on the subject. Pensioners, in particular, still remember when there were no safety nets in Japanese society before the Second World War and when to have no savings for old age would have been considered a calamitous situation.

Tamura Kotaro leads a group of 65 lawmakers of the LDP and has proposed to Prime Minister Aso Taro that the government should inject some of its abundant liquidity into both European and US banks, which are finding themselves short of cash, and buy up distressed corporate assets at the lowest prices. Much as a landlord who has abundant equity should buy up repossessed houses at knock-down prices, and with the Japanese government being in a strong position because of its capital reserves, he believes that Japan should buy corporate assets cheaply and reap the huge financial benefits in ten years' time. The Japanese, traditionally known as a people with a long-term view, would find this idea convincing, especially in light of the USA being their largest export market. Thus, to assist in rebuilding the US economy, so that American consumers begin spending once more on their usual large scale, can only benefit Japan in the long term. The downside is that the Japanese are risk averse in their behaviour and are natural fiscal conservatives because of their history of having to be self-reliant and prudent.

Even in the 1990s, when Japanese banks were crumbling under the weight of bad loans and debt, the Japanese public were against a publicly backed bail-out for the banks. Added to this, although Japan is the second largest economy in the world, with foreign reserves second only to China at $US 1.9 trillion, it also has the highest public debt in the world, which amounts to 182 per cent of its GDP, compared to roughly 36 per cent in the USA. Japan also has the longest-living populace in the world while having one of the lowest birth rates. Therefore, demands on the state for pensions and medical treatment for the elderly are constantly rising, while the number of young people in employment is diminishing. Consequently, while Tamura's idea is quite compelling in many respects, the administration of Aso Taro is not acting on his advice.

Prime Minister Aso Taro, who comes from a long line of well-connected ancestors, both in politics and in the imperial family – his sister Nobuko married a Crown Prince, has been losing popularity and has been attacked in the media for his lavish lifestyle. Especially during a period of economic downturn, a dim view is held by the population of Mr Aso's visits on a regular basis to the most expensive bars and restaurants in Tokyo, where he spends hundreds of yen. His predecessor, Mr Fukuda, celebrated in this way for maybe the first week after his election but then returned to a much more modest lifestyle. Despite his lavish lifestyle, the Japanese people will forgive Mr Aso if he is able, with his cabinet, to turn around the fortunes of the Japanese economy by reducing the debt, solving the pension and medical crisis for the elderly, reforming the tax system and making a wise decision concerning the previously mentioned refuelling issue in the Indian Ocean, in addition to continuing the work of former Prime Minister Koizumi concerning structural reform. Whether he will be assisted in any way by Mr Koizumi remains to be seen, as the latter recently stated that he will not be standing for any public office again but has not ruled out activity behind the scenes. It is not clear whether Mr Aso will be able to deliver on all the above or any part of it before the next general election in September 2009. Whether the DPJ President, Mr Ozawa, is elected on the basis of a need for 'change' following the lead in the recent US elections, and/or Mr Ozawa's long-standing connections to former Prime Minister Koizumi, remains to be seen. A drop in the price of fuel globally, which has occurred during the Aso administration, can only serve to assist Prime Minister Aso's bid for re-election.

The way forward

The political future prospects of Japan are crucial, with a general election only about a year away. The type of leadership chosen will decide whether the Koizumi administration's structural reforms will stall completely with great detriment to the recovery of the Japanese economy and progress made to date, or whether it will move forward. Both parties in the meantime could choose new leaders. The popularity of the current President of the DPJ, Ozawa Ichiro, and the quality of his ideas in continuing the Koizumi reforms and for revitalizing the economy and dealing with the problems of the ageing population, will determine whether he will be re-elected as the next Prime Minister of Japan. This will also depend on whether the traditionally risk-averse Japanese people are willing to make a change and give him a chance. Tax reform will be a crucial issue for fiscal year 2009. Pension expenditure is to be increased, which will be welcomed by the ageing population, but calls for a higher consumption tax to cover it will not be welcomed, as this tax has caused violent opposition from the people in the past (see Chapter 1). Taxes on petrol and other fuels may be the answer, or increased economic growth because of successful innovation that is being encouraged by the government.

Current decline in innovation

The great strides made in Japan concerning innovation in relation to venture creation through TLOs, IP drives and other vehicles of innovation mentioned in preceding chapters are all declining since the return to political protectionism, conservatism and confusion following the final days of the Koizumi administration and the beginning of the Abe government. Although the numbers of university start-ups, for example, are growing, the number of successful ventures is declining rapidly and those in existence are deteriorating severely. In the Appendix of this book, the initiation and progression of the new start-ups can be seen clearly, with an updated current chart of the situation of university start-ups in Japan by Professor Nishizawa Akio of Tohoku University. The promotion of IP has slowed, but the creation of new IP highways, as discussed in Chapter 4, is still continuing apace because of efforts by the JPO and the business community, which requires them to operate globally with success, which means patenting and related IP and protecting those patents and IPR.

Hope in the new BOJ Governor

By all accounts, the new Governor of the BOJ, Shirakawa Masaaki, will instil confidence in foreign investors in Japan. Mr Shirakawa has the academic ability for analysis and is a monetary policy expert, in addition to having great knowledge about the administration of financial organs, reform of the settlement system and analysis of bonds and securitized markets. He is also the right person to facilitate global connections, having built many relationships with central bankers of other countries, especially when stationed in New York.

Like former Prime Minister Koizumi, Mr Shirakawa is an advocate of deregulation, leaving the private sector to handle its own affairs. His free market persuasion may be attributable to his study at the University of Chicago, which is a school well known for its free market economics. He has had pressure on him to lower interest rates in 2008, especially in light of the BOJ's *tankan* survey, as mentioned in Chapter 1, which shows general unease in the financial markets. However, in the current situation there seems to be no need to push any lower the BOJ's short-term benchmark rate, which is at present 0.5 per cent, as that move would run the risk of causing asset bubbles to form again in the future.

It is suggested that Mr Shirakawa would only tend to lower interest rates in the event of a crisis, whereby American financial institutions' collapse would cause major Japanese banks to also suffer serious damage, such as raising funds on the inter-bank market. In such a dire case, the BOJ under Mr Shirakawa would most likely lower interest rates and expand market liquidity to a high degree.[5]

In August 2008, the BOJ left the current low interest rates unchanged and warned of possible recession, as the economy contracted by 0.6 per cent in the second quarter of 2008. In June 2008, Japan's basic inflation rate reached a high of 1.9 per cent, which has not been seen for a decade, and inflation is attributed to higher materials, food and energy costs, which lowered corporate profits and inhibited consumer spending. Consumer prices rose for a ninth straight month. The price of goods traded between companies, or the wholesale inflation rate, jumped to 7.1 per cent, which has been the highest increase since the 8.1 per cent rise in January 1981, when Japan was experiencing the second oil price shock. Business investment and strong export sales were key to Japan's economic recovery in the recessionary years of the 1990s and there is concern that companies may reduce spending on factory building and new equipment to cope with higher costs.

However, it was hoped that a drop in the price of crude oil and a number of other commodities would provide a breathing space for Japanese manufacturers and lower wholesale inflation by the end of 2008 and the beginning of 2009. Raw material prices soared to 48.6 per cent in July 2008, while the prices of finished goods rose by only 1.6 per cent. Prices surged 43.6 per cent for petroleum and coal products, 26.7 per cent for iron and steel and 8.1 per cent for electricity, gas and water.[6]

Within this context of the Japanese economy facing a harsh environment, the new BOJ Governor will have to be wary of political considerations, as the wrangling over his appointment showed that the central bank is not completely independent of the Japanese government and that its future is linked to that of whatever new administration will come to the fore in the next general election. Importantly, will the new Japanese administration govern with authority and continue the essential Koizumi-inspired structural reforms and IP drive?

Privatization of the Development Bank of Japan

In line with the move towards globalization that began in earnest during the Koizumi administration along with the IP drive, the DBJ, which was a purely government institution, became a private profit-driven bank on 1 October 2008. The DBJ previously had a role akin to the European Bank of Reconstruction, which, after the Second World War, served to revitalize the Japanese economy after widespread devastation. The DBJ was reconstituted to assist SMEs in particular, which had been damaged by the severe decade-long stagnation, deflation and recession that the Japanese economy experienced in the 1990s, through a unique policy that demonstrated the vital link between the rise of the importance of intangible assets in the form of IP and new growth in the economy. The DBJ had a policy of using IP, such as patents and trademarks, as collateral against loans.[7]

The DBJ, prior to the new privatization, had difficulty in implementing policies and loans because it was often hindered by red tape and bureaucracy. This often took the form of bureaucratic DBJ employees forming and sitting on committees of TLOs and SMEs and arranging the timetables and contents of meetings, meaning that no progress could be made until the next meeting, which frustrated, at times, the efforts of the entrepreneurs running the enterprises.

Privatization initiated during the Koizumi years is enabling the DBJ to act with greater transparency and less bureaucratic interference, and also within the context of globalized markets, giving TLOs and SMEs the assistance they require to profit using market forces worldwide. The Japanese long-term perspective remains but, as the DBJ President, Mr Murofushi Minoru, noted, within the context 'of applying financial expertise to design the future'.[8]

Future relations with Japan's direct neighbours

As have many East Asian and Southeast Asian countries, Japan has relied on the USA for security. If the economy of the USA shrinks or the new US president elect shies away from foreign policy responsibilities in line with professed tendencies towards trade protectionism to keep jobs in America, Japan will have to rethink its security policies. In the worst-case scenario of Americans turning against buying products from abroad, the new prime minister will have to do more than continue structural reforms and will have to reorganize the whole basis of the Japanese economy.[9] A move towards promoting greater trading relations between the countries of Japan, China and India can only assist the region, along with building cross-border highways that link all the countries of Asia.

It is predicted that, by 2030, China's economy will become five times as large and India's will double. If China and India join economically, the entire balance of power and economic might will shift to Asia and dwarf both Japan and the USA. However, such an alliance is not a foregone conclusion and neither are the economic predictions of growth in China and India.

IP infrastructure

Two areas in which Japan can contribute in the Asian region and assist in furthering Asian regional cooperation, which will serve to strengthen economic and political ties, are the building of infrastructure and the promotion of IP highways. These two areas can be integrally linked as new buildings, highways connecting all the parts of Asia, and marine infrastructure such as ports will all promote greater enterprise, which will give rise to more IP as new products that require patenting are created to develop the new infrastructure. The IP highway will serve as a uniting force in that countries throughout the region can agree on ways of simplifying cross-border examinations for patenting and infringement prosecution. IP design patenting can be extended to apply to new infrastructural buildings, products and designs, creating a new category of IP infrastructure that will not only give Asian countries pride, but also attach added value to their infrastructure, which will increase wealth and cooperation in the Asian region. Japan has the most advanced technical knowledge and infrastructure in the region and, along with development of the IP highway with South Korea, can encourage greater economic and social relations with its neighbours through the concept of value-added IP infrastructure, which can be implemented in a tangible manner. Business can take a lead in these IP infrastructure developments, but the Japanese and other Asian governments must be careful not to block these positive developments through a lack of political vision.

Appendix

Growth of TLOs and spin-offs, 1989–2007

Professor Nishizawa Akio, Deputy Director of the New Industry Hatchery Centre, Tohoku University, Sendai, Japan, explains very thoroughly over the following pages, by means of self-explanatory graphs and figures, the mixed success of technical licensing organizations and new-venture spin-offs and the management of IPR between universities and industry in Japan. Professor Nishizawa also suggests the way forward for greater success in these university ventures.

New challenges for the Japanese national universities in IPR management and spin-off ventures

Nishizawa Akio
Professor, Graduate School of Economics and Management,
Deputy Director, New Industry Hatchery Center,
Tohoku University, Sendai, Japan

Losing Japanese industrial competitiveness

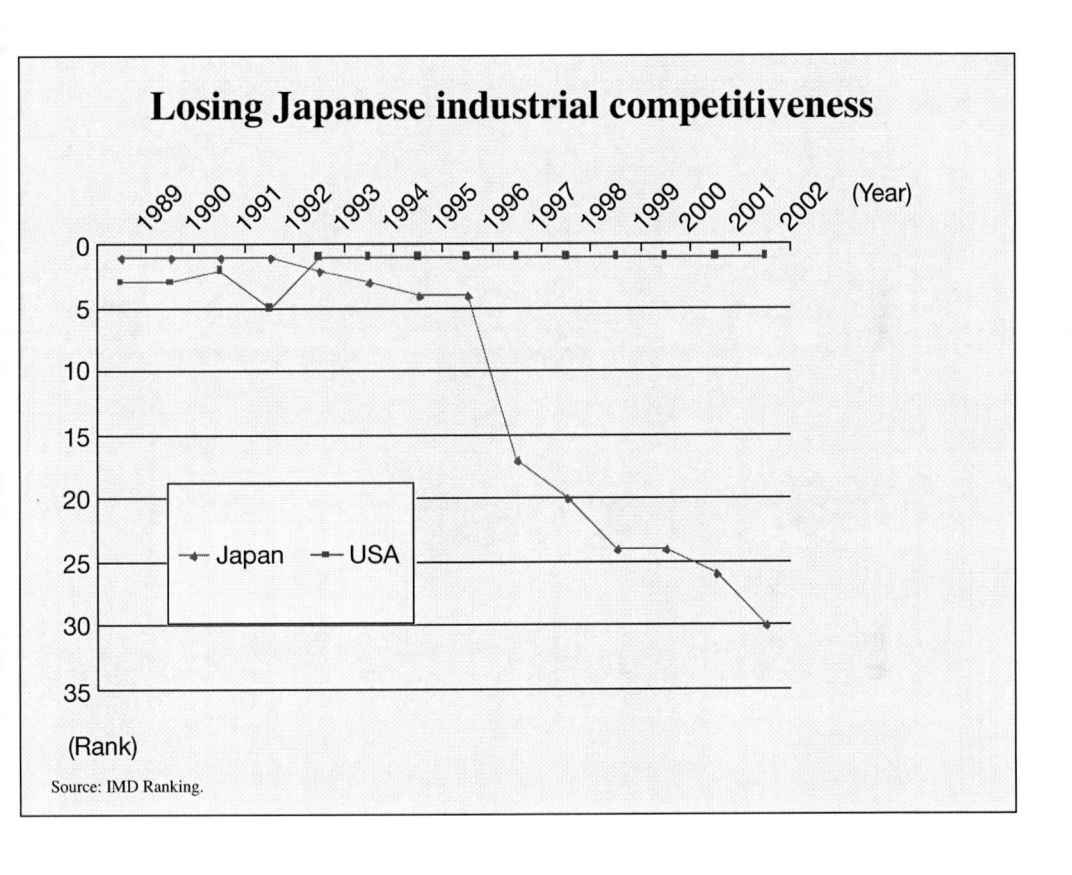

Source: IMD Ranking.

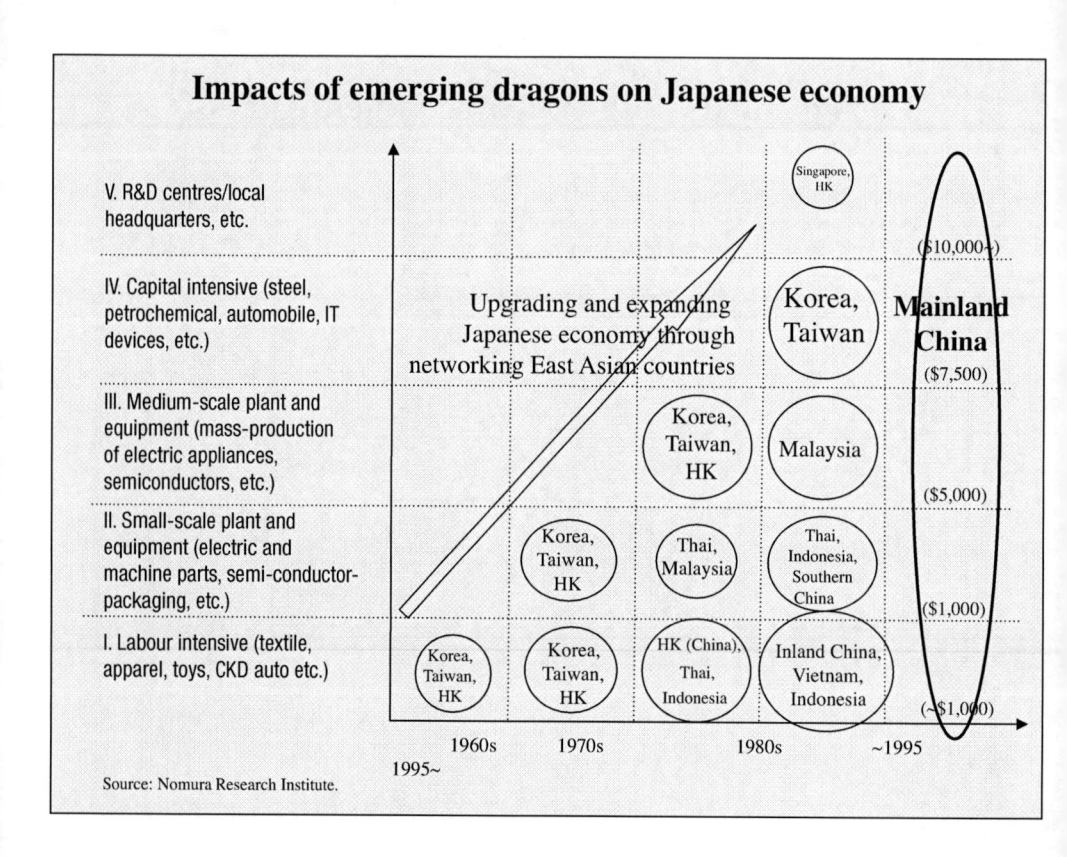

Appendix

Impacts of emerging dragons on Japanese economy

Category	1960s	1970s	1980s	~1995	1995~
V. R&D centres/local headquarters, etc.			Singapore, HK		($10,000+)
IV. Capital intensive (steel, petrochemical, automobile, IT devices, etc.)				Korea, Taiwan	**Mainland China** ($7,500)
III. Medium-scale plant and equipment (mass-production of electric appliances, semiconductors, etc.)			Korea, Taiwan, HK	Malaysia	($5,000)
II. Small-scale plant and equipment (electric and machine parts, semi-conductor packaging, etc.)		Korea, Taiwan, HK	Thai, Malaysia	Thai, Indonesia, Southern China	($1,000)
I. Labour intensive (textile, apparel, toys, CKD auto etc.)	Korea, Taiwan, HK	Korea, Taiwan, HK	HK (China), Thai, Indonesia	Inland China, Vietnam, Indonesia	(~$1,000)

Upgrading and expanding Japanese economy through networking East Asian countries

Source: Nomura Research Institute.

Appendix 111

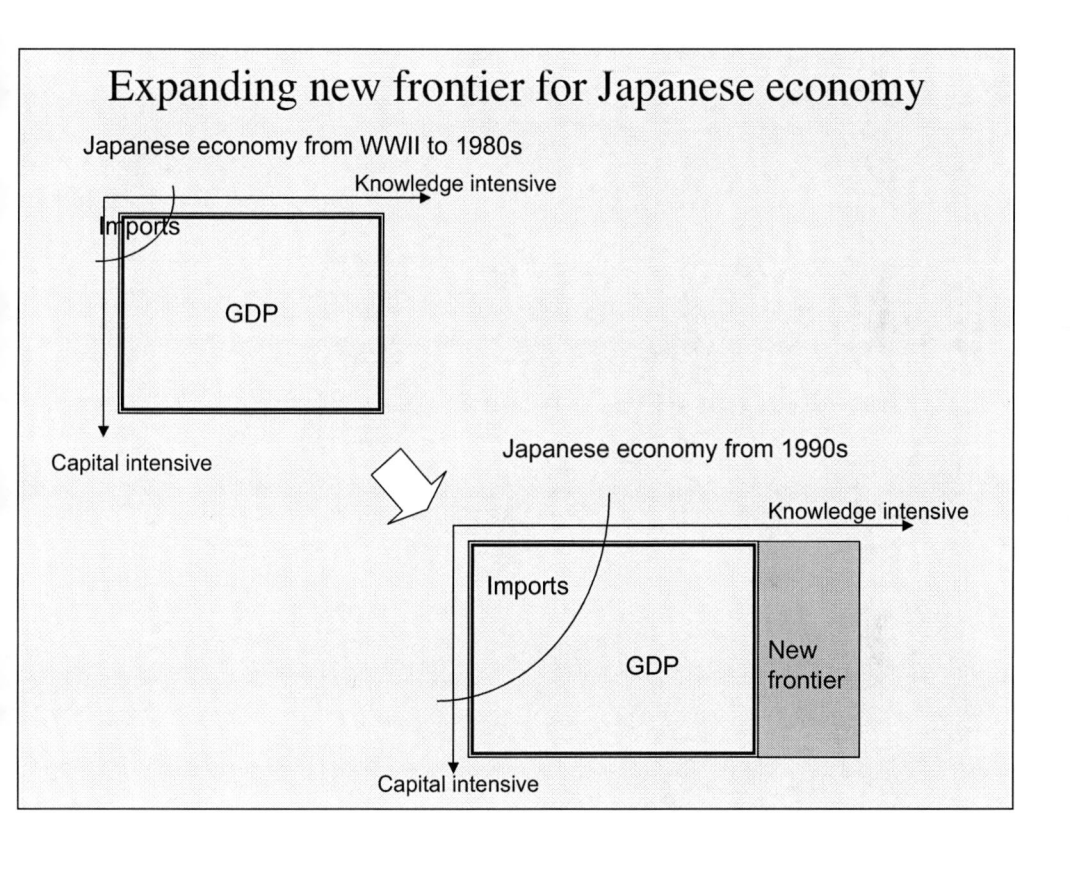

Expanding new frontier for Japanese economy

Japanese economy from WWII to 1980s

Knowledge intensive →

Imports

GDP

Capital intensive ↓

Japanese economy from 1990s

Knowledge intensive →

Imports

GDP | New frontier

Capital intensive ↓

Background:
A similar situation to that in the USA of the late 1970s

Japan chases similar strategies to those taken in the USA in the early 1980s:

Pursuing new collaborations between industry and academia

Japanese economy does need structural change to be rejuvenated through:

- changing from follow-through to break-through;
- changing from centralized to decentralized;
- changing from government-guided to market-oriented;
- changing from big businesses with scale of economy to entrepreneurial ventures with scope of economy;
- changing from capital-labour intensive to knowledge intensive.

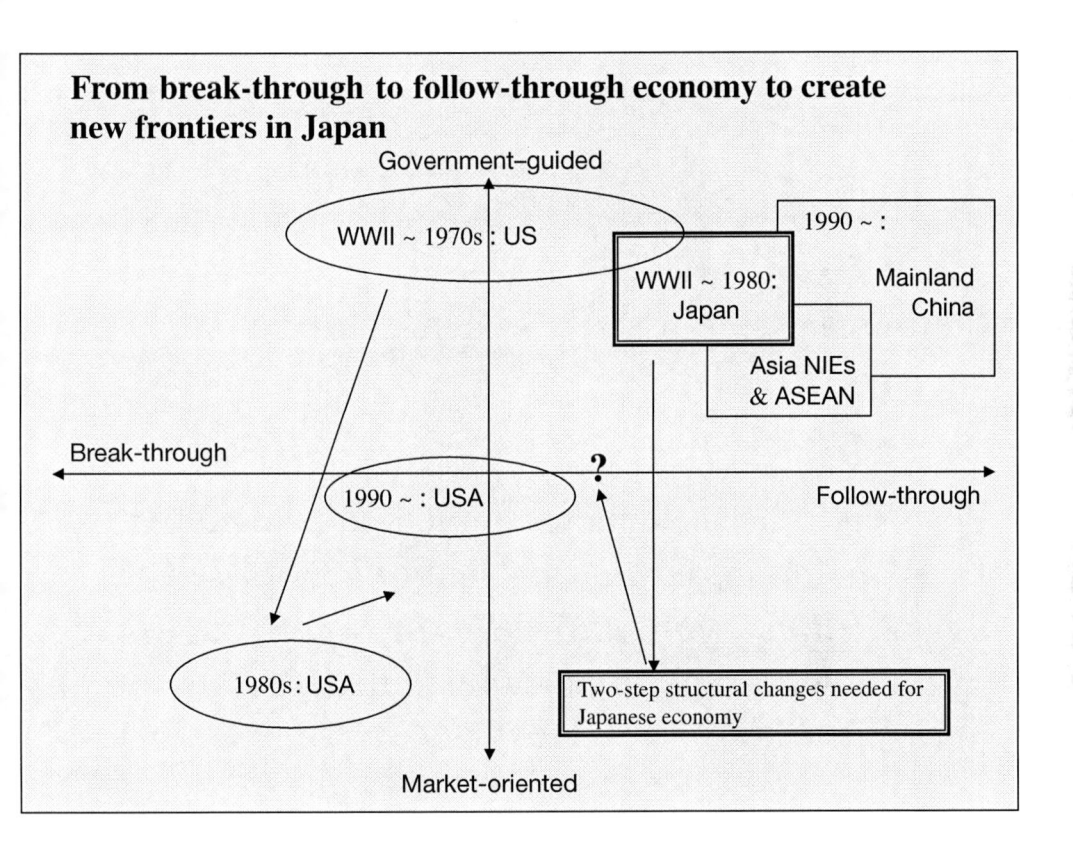

From break-through to follow-through economy to create new frontiers in Japan

- Government–guided / Market-oriented (vertical axis)
- Break-through / Follow-through (horizontal axis)

- WWII ~ 1970s: US
- WWII ~ 1980: Japan
- 1990 ~ : Mainland China
- Asia NIEs & ASEAN
- 1990 ~ : USA
- 1980s: USA
- Two-step structural changes needed for Japanese economy

1998 to 2004:

Preliminary tech-transfer system started at the universities in Japan.

➡

Please refer to the chapter in the book edited by Dr Ruth Taplin, *Exploiting Patent Rights and a New Climate for Innovation in Japan*, published by the Intellectual Property Institute (IPI), UK in March, 2003.

Appendix 117

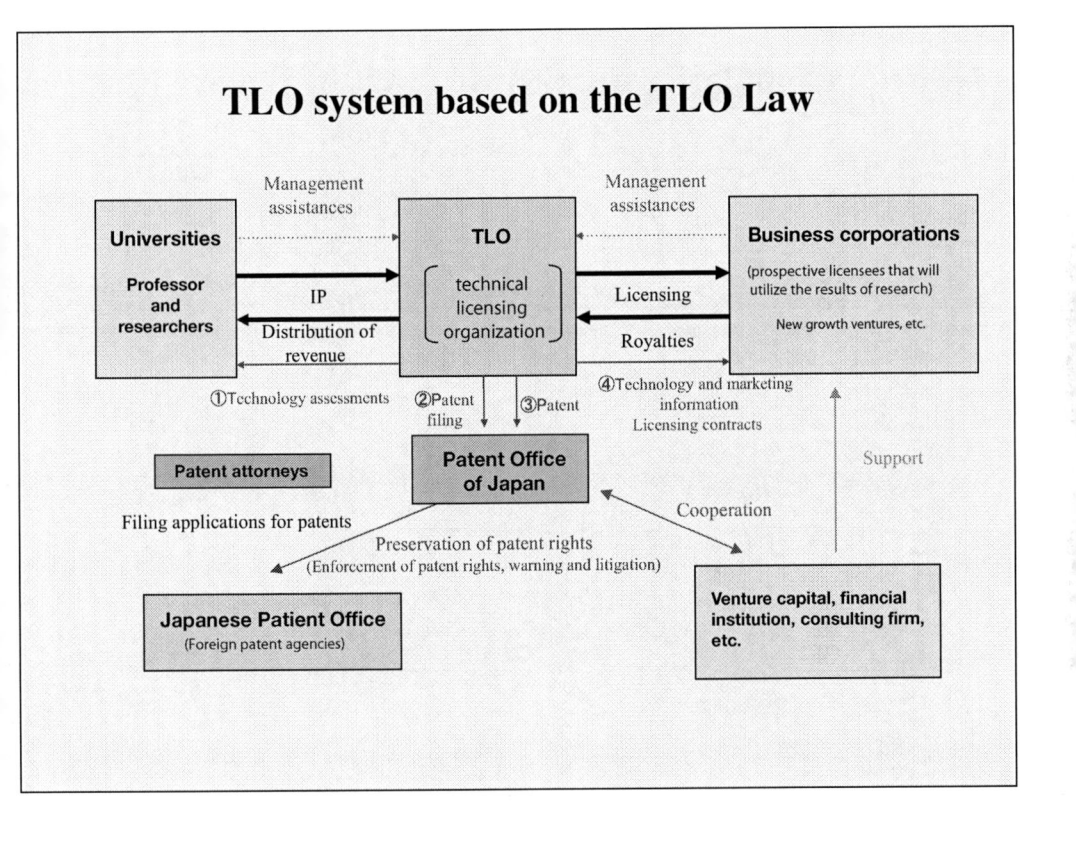

TLO system based on the TLO Law

Universities — Professor and researchers
- Management assistances ┄┄→ TLO
- IP → TLO
- TLO → Distribution of revenue

TLO (technical licensing organization)
- Licensing → Business corporations
- Royalties ← Business corporations

Business corporations (prospective licensees that will utilize the results of research) — New growth ventures, etc.
- Management assistances ┄┄→ Business corporations

① Technology assessments ② Patent filing ③ Patent ④ Technology and marketing information / Licensing contracts

Patent attorneys

Patent Office of Japan

Filing applications for patents

Preservation of patent rights
(Enforcement of patent rights, warning and litigation)

Japanese Patient Office
(Foreign patent agencies)

Cooperation

Venture capital, financial institution, consulting firm, etc.

Support

Cumulative number of TLOs in Japan

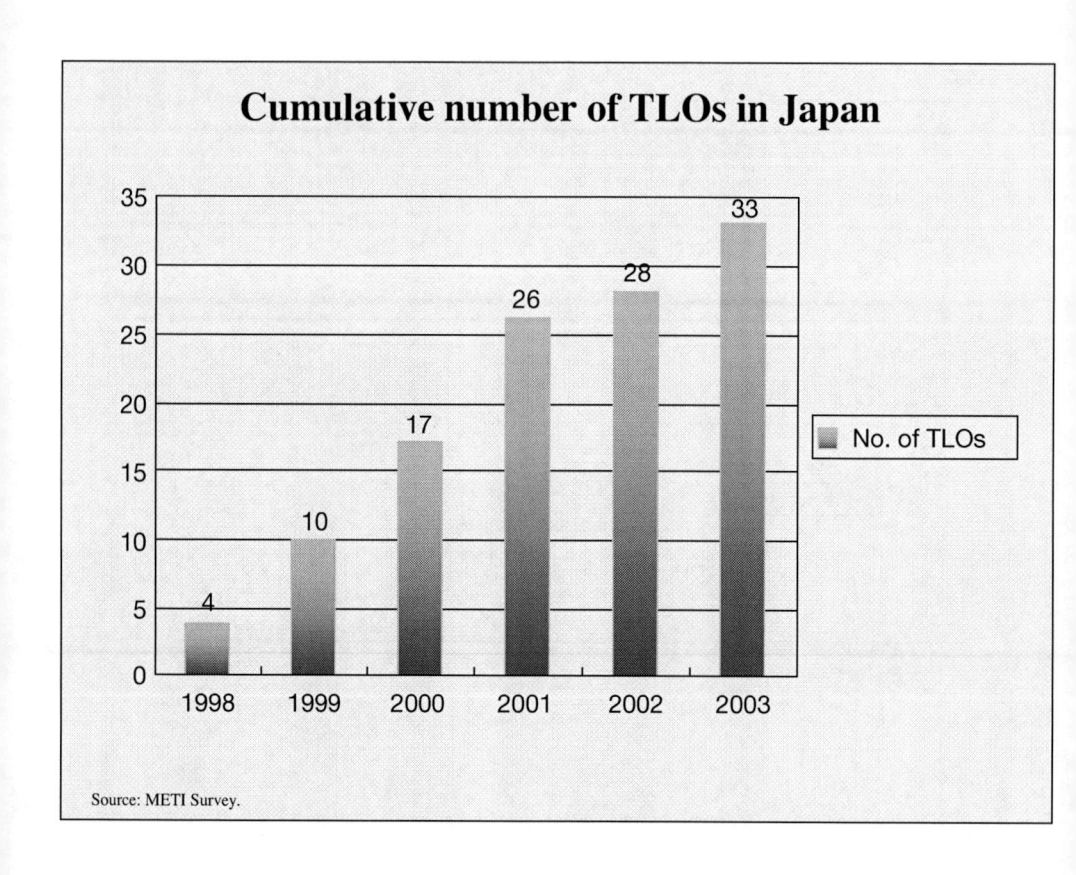

Year	No. of TLOs
1998	4
1999	10
2000	17
2001	26
2002	28
2003	33

Source: METI Survey.

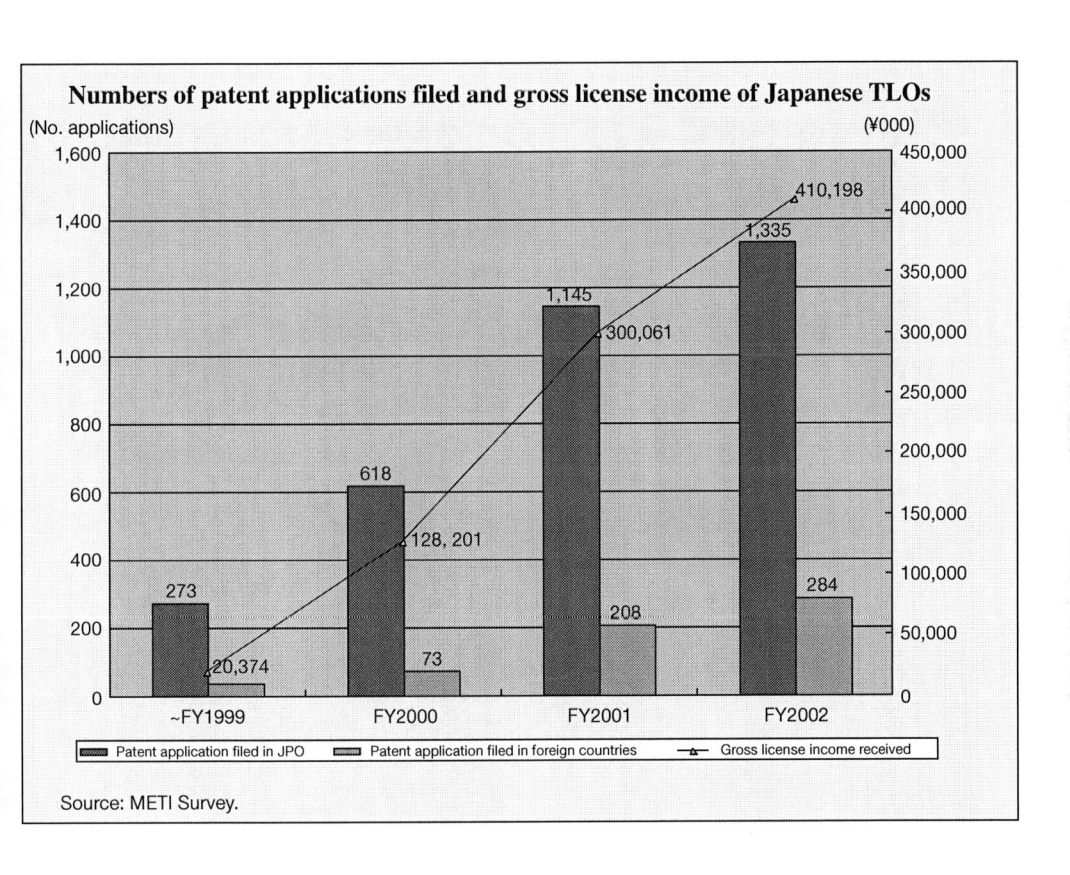

Numbers of patent applications filed and gross license income of Japanese TLOs

	~FY1999	FY2000	FY2001	FY2002
Patent application filed in JPO	273	618	1,145	1,335
Patent application filed in foreign countries		73	208	284
Gross license income received (¥000)	20,374	128,201	300,061	410,198

Source: METI Survey.

Revenue of TLO on average (FY2002)

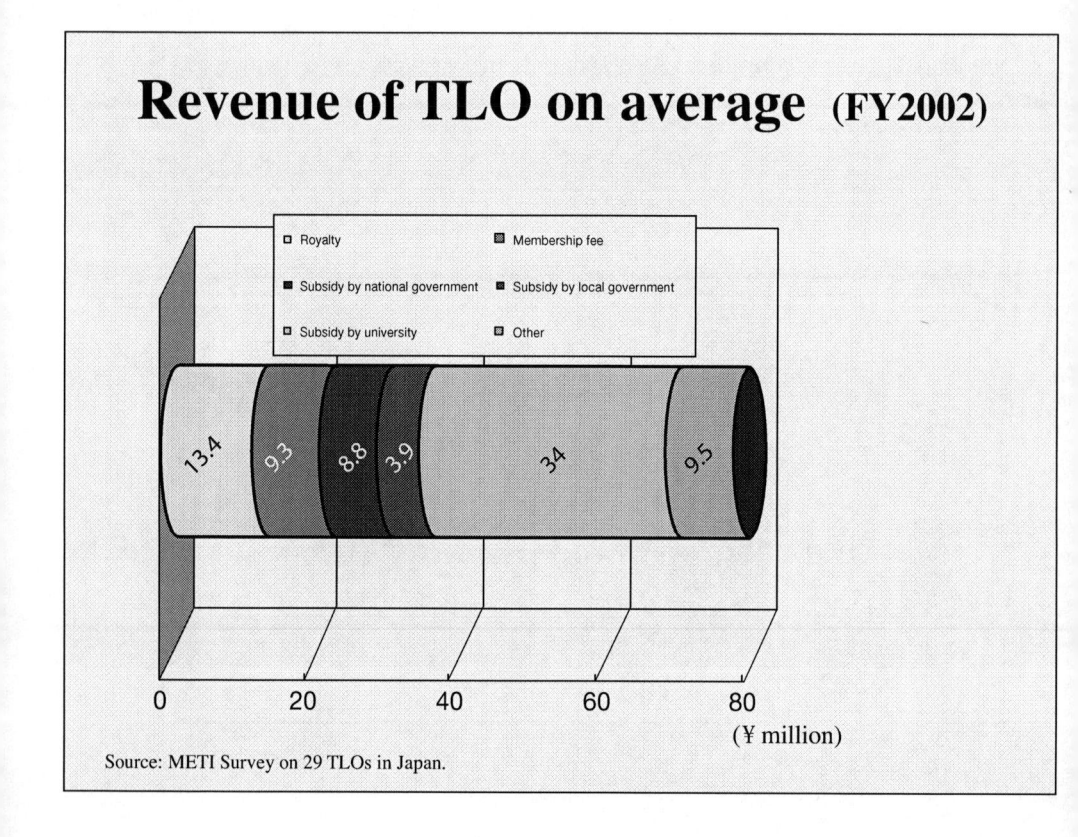

- Royalty: 13.4
- Membership fee: 9.3
- Subsidy by national government: 8.8
- Subsidy by local government: 3.9
- Subsidy by university: 34
- Other: 9.5

(¥ million)

Source: METI Survey on 29 TLOs in Japan.

Cost of TLO on average (FY2002)

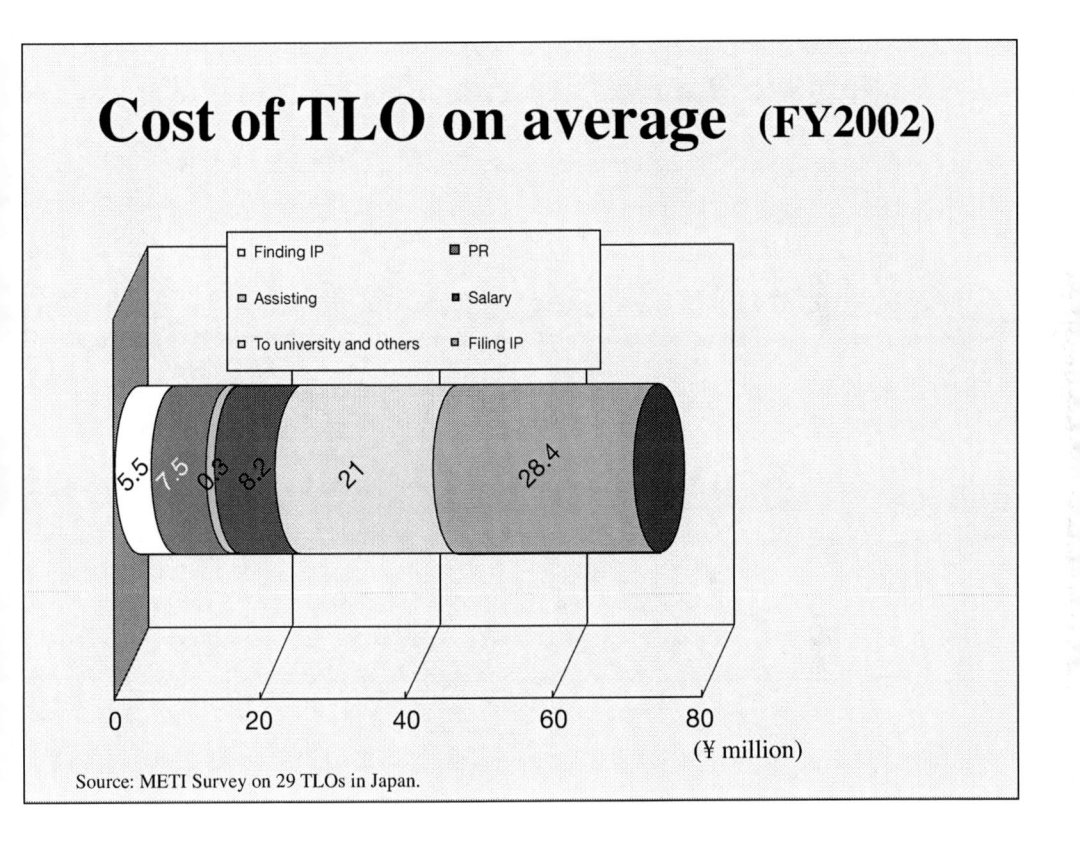

- Finding IP
- PR
- Assisting
- Salary
- To university and others
- Filing IP

5.5 | 7.5 | 0.3 | 8.2 | 21 | 28.4

(¥ million)

Source: METI Survey on 29 TLOs in Japan.

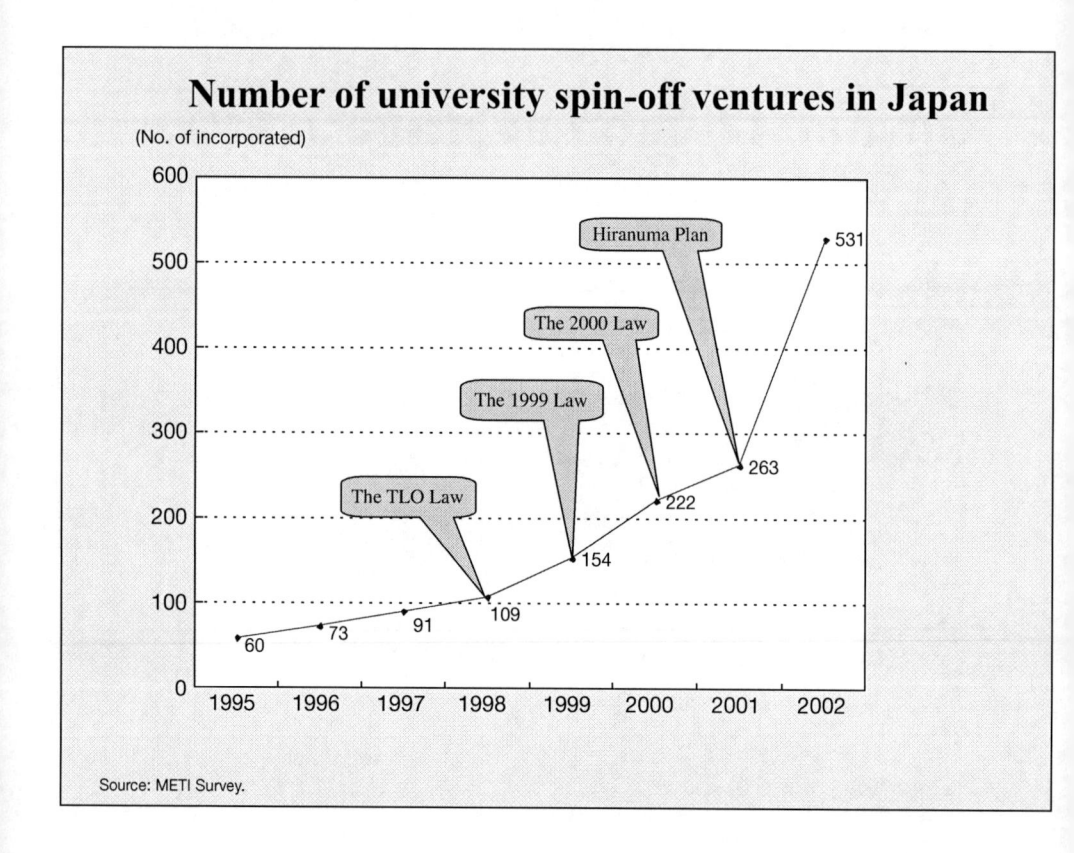

Number of university spin-off ventures in Japan

(No. of incorporated)

- 1995: 60
- 1996: 73
- 1997: 91
- 1998: 109 — The TLO Law
- 1999: 154 — The 1999 Law
- 2000: 222 — The 2000 Law
- 2001: 263 — Hiranuma Plan
- 2002: 531

Source: METI Survey.

From 2004:

Japanese national universities structurally changed from being a part of the national government to becoming independent institutions with legal entities that can own the IPRs and transfer by themselves.

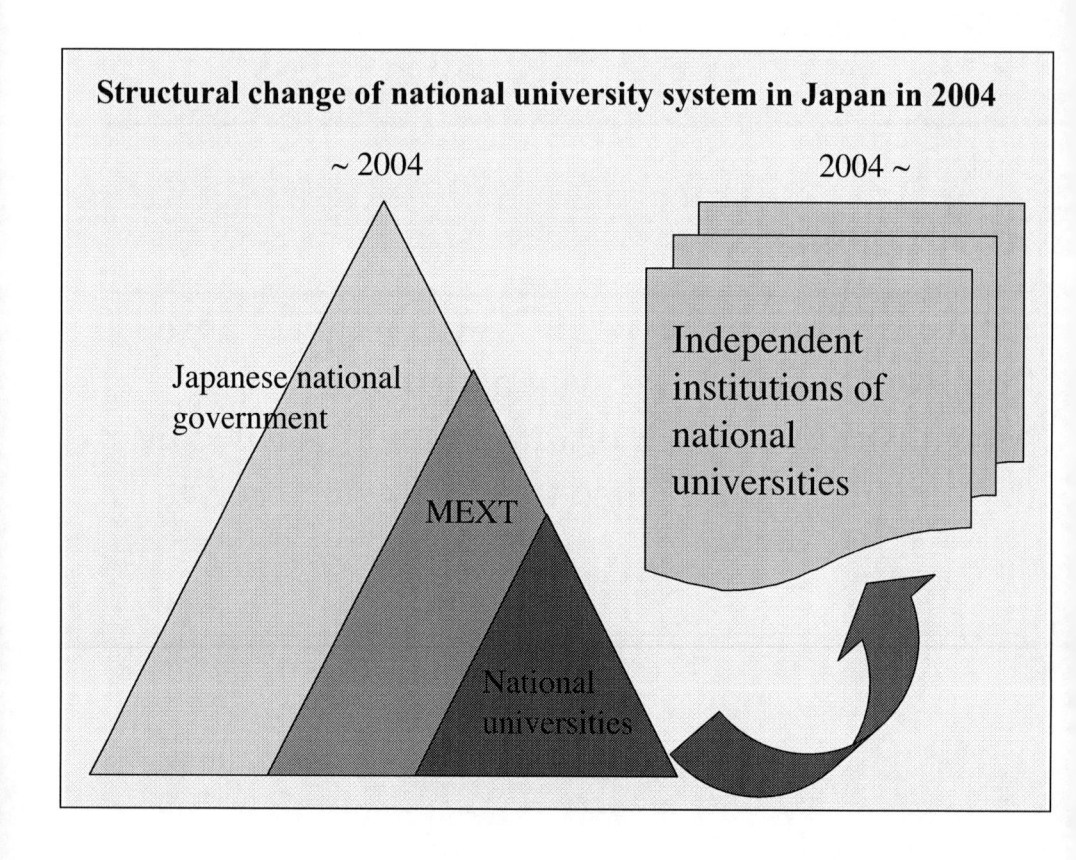

Structural change of national university system in Japan in 2004

~ 2004

Japanese national government

MEXT

National universities

2004 ~

Independent institutions of national universities

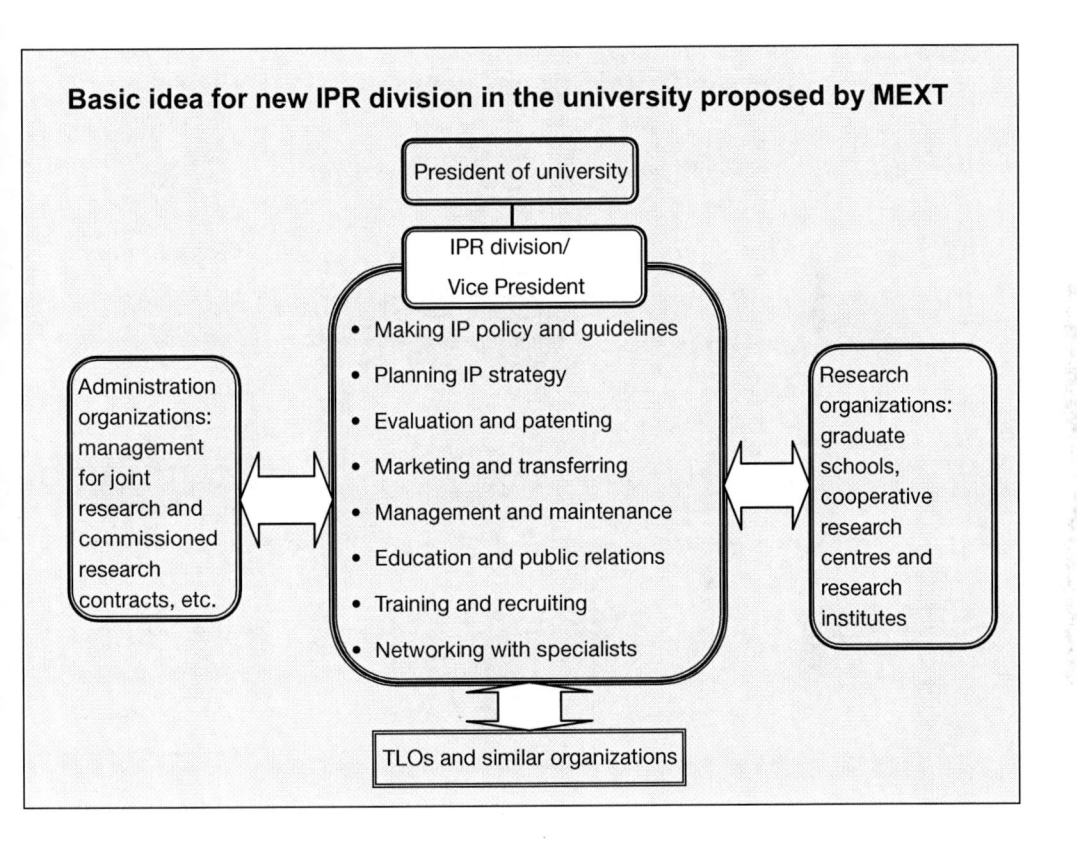

Basic idea for new IPR division in the university proposed by MEXT

President of university

IPR division/ Vice President

- Making IP policy and guidelines
- Planning IP strategy
- Evaluation and patenting
- Marketing and transferring
- Management and maintenance
- Education and public relations
- Training and recruiting
- Networking with specialists

Administration organizations: management for joint research and commissioned research contracts, etc.

Research organizations: graduate schools, cooperative research centres and research institutes

TLOs and similar organizations

34 university IPR divisions awarded by MEXT

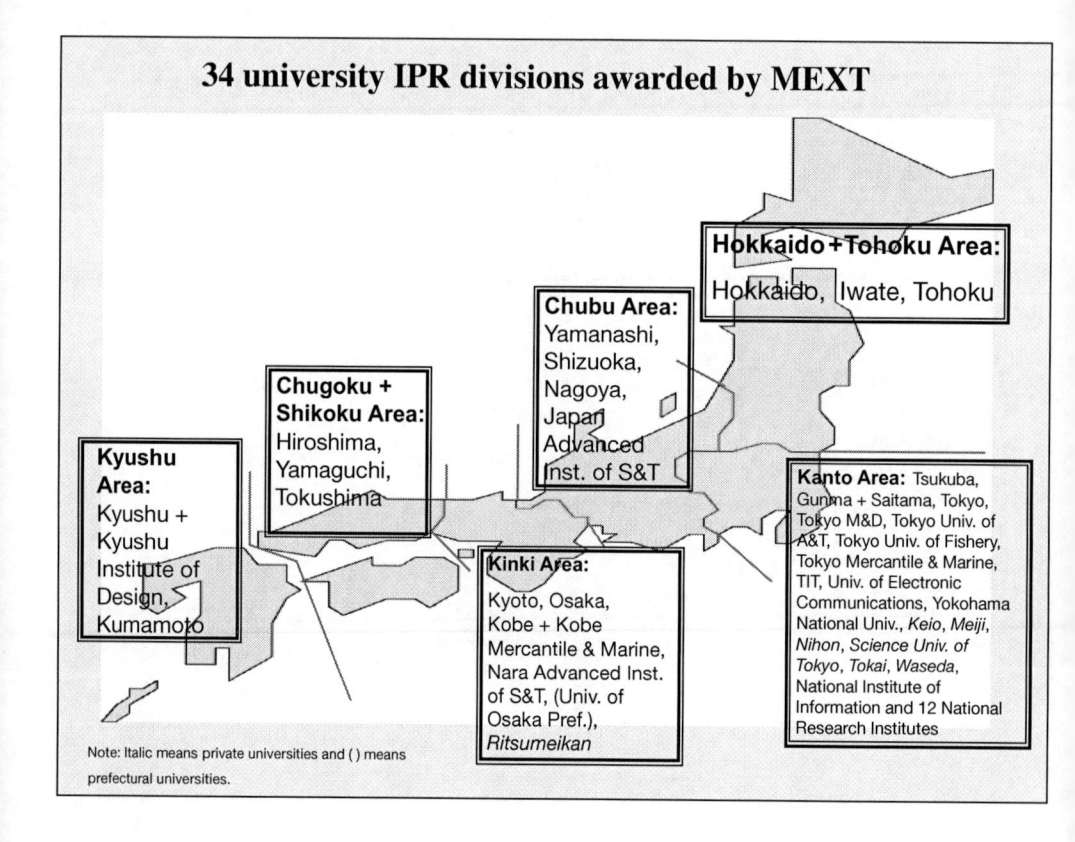

Hokkaido + Tohoku Area: Hokkaido, Iwate, Tohoku

Chubu Area: Yamanashi, Shizuoka, Nagoya, Japan Advanced Inst. of S&T

Chugoku + Shikoku Area: Hiroshima, Yamaguchi, Tokushima

Kyushu Area: Kyushu + Kyushu Institute of Design, Kumamoto

Kinki Area: Kyoto, Osaka, Kobe + Kobe Mercantile & Marine, Nara Advanced Inst. of S&T, (Univ. of Osaka Pref.), *Ritsumeikan*

Kanto Area: Tsukuba, Gunma + Saitama, Tokyo, Tokyo M&D, Tokyo Univ. of A&T, Tokyo Univ. of Fishery, Tokyo Mercantile & Marine, TIT, Univ. of Electronic Communications, Yokohama National Univ., *Keio, Meiji, Nihon, Science Univ. of Tokyo, Tokai, Waseda*, National Institute of Information and 12 National Research Institutes

Note: Italic means private universities and ( ) means prefectural universities.

The problems to be solved:
Again, there is a need for more structural change

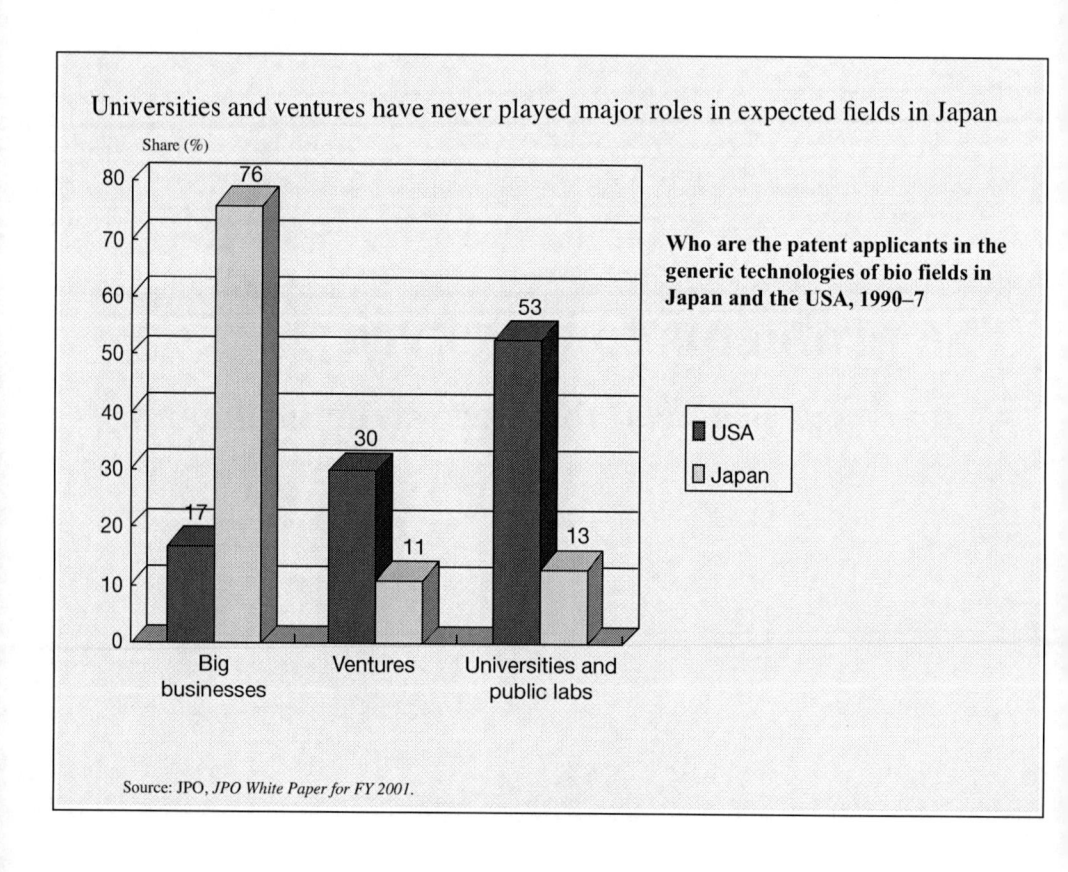

Universities and ventures have never played major roles in expected fields in Japan

Who are the patent applicants in the generic technologies of bio fields in Japan and the USA, 1990–7

	USA	Japan
Big businesses	17	76
Ventures	30	11
Universities and public labs	53	13

Source: JPO, *JPO White Paper for FY 2001*.

Appendix 129

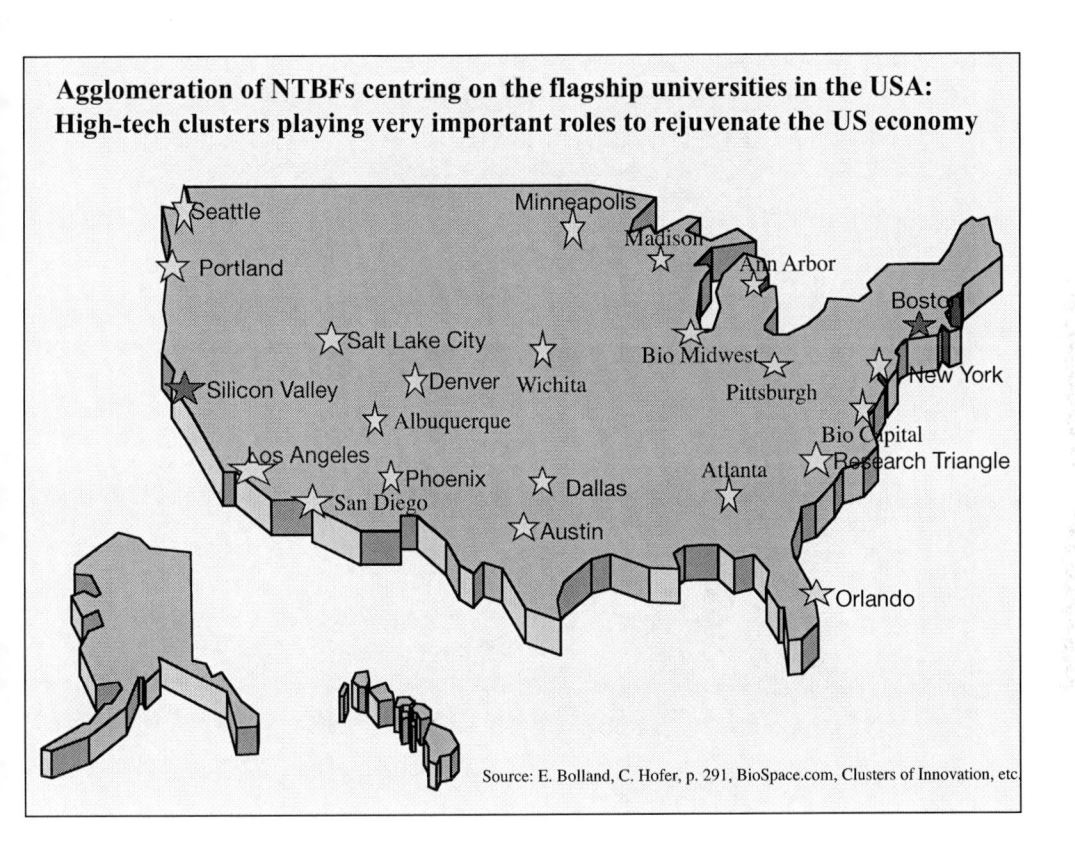

Agglomeration of NTBFs centring on the flagship universities in the USA: High-tech clusters playing very important roles to rejuvenate the US economy

☆ Seattle
☆ Portland
☆ Minneapolis
☆ Madison
☆ Ann Arbor
★ Boston
☆ Salt Lake City
☆ Bio Midwest
☆ New York
★ Silicon Valley
☆ Denver
Wichita
☆ Pittsburgh
☆ Albuquerque
☆ Bio Capital
☆ Los Angeles
☆ Phoenix
☆ Dallas
☆ Atlanta
☆ Research Triangle
☆ San Diego
☆ Austin
☆ Orlando

Source: E. Bolland, C. Hofer, p. 291, BioSpace.com, Clusters of Innovation, etc.

Can knowledge clusters in Japan awarded by MEXT play the same roles as in the USA?

- SAPPORO
- KYOTO
- KANSAI-KOUIKI
- NAGANO-UEDA
- SENDAI
- HIROSHIMA
- KYUSYU-KOUIKI
- HAMAMATSU
- TAKAMATSU
- KANSAI-BUNKA-GAKUJUTSU-KENKYU-TOSHI

Appendix 131

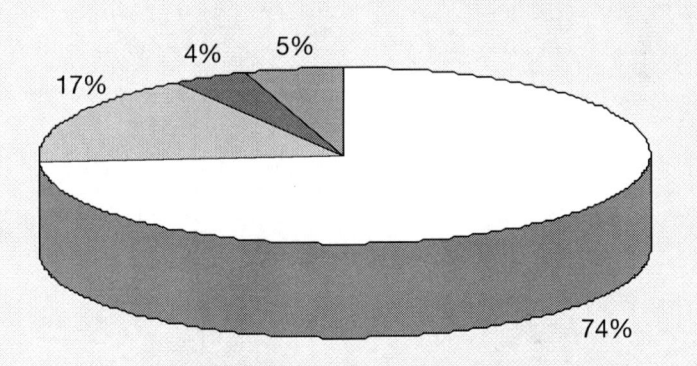

Regional distribution of patent agents and attorneys, showing lack of specialists in local areas in Japan (as of the end of 2000)

- 17%
- 4%
- 5%
- 74%

□ Tokyo area　▨ Osaka area　▨ Nagoya area　▨ Other areas

Source: JPO, *JPO Annual Report 2001*.

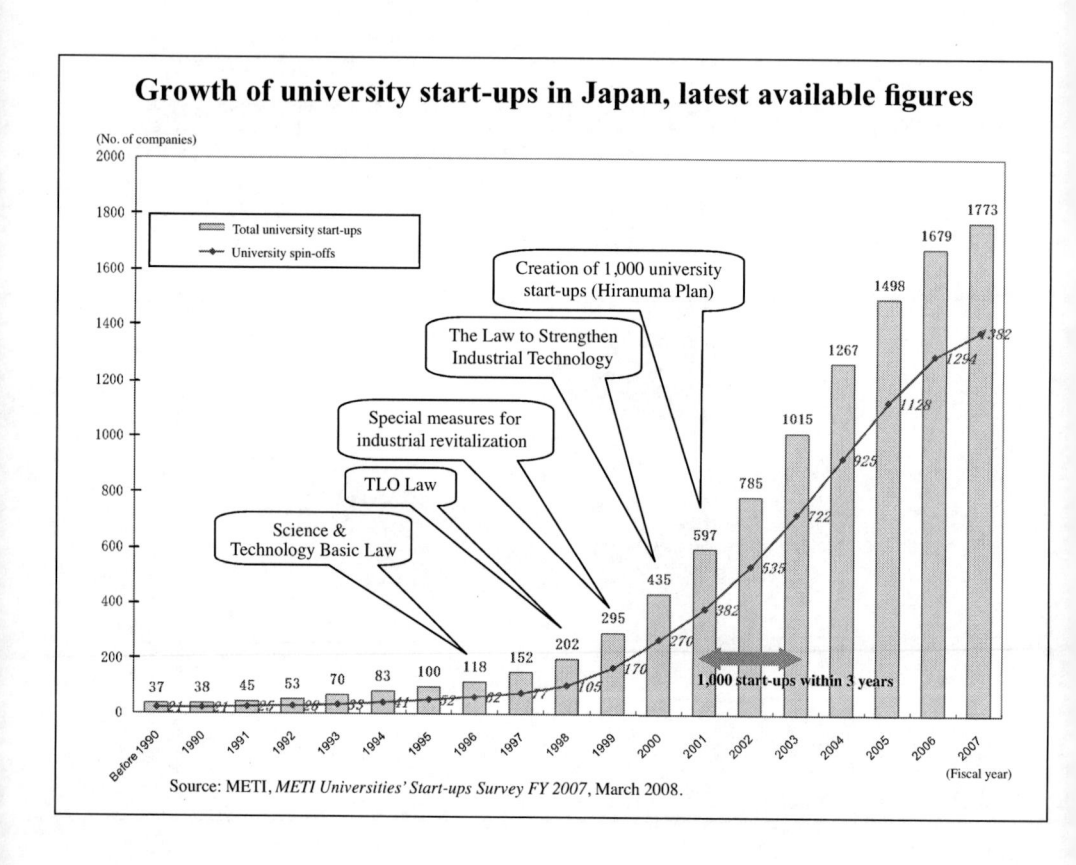

Growth of university start-ups in Japan, latest available figures

Total university start-ups by fiscal year: 37 (Before 1990), 38 (1990), 45 (1991), 53 (1992), 70 (1993), 83 (1994), 100 (1995), 118 (1996), 152 (1997), 202 (1998), 295 (1999), 435 (2000), 597 (2001), 785 (2002), 1015 (2003), 1267 (2004), 1498 (2005), 1679 (2006), 1773 (2007).

University spin-offs: 21 (Before 1990), 21 (1990), 26 (1991), 28 (1992), 35 (1993), 41 (1994), 52 (1995), 62 (1996), 77 (1997), 105 (1998), 170 (1999), 270 (2000), 382 (2001), 535 (2002), 722 (2003), 925 (2004), 1128 (2005), 1294 (2006), 1382 (2007).

Annotations:
- Science & Technology Basic Law
- TLO Law
- Special measures for industrial revitalization
- The Law to Strengthen Industrial Technology
- Creation of 1,000 university start-ups (Hiranuma Plan)
- 1,000 start-ups within 3 years

Source: METI, *METI Universities' Start-ups Survey FY 2007*, March 2008.

In conclusion, the keys for the success of the new challenges to Japanese national universities may depend upon:

- whether universities, especially national universities, one of Japan's major research players, can construct their IPR management systems with clear missions and policies;
- whether Japanese big businesses will change their R&D strategies from closed to open to enhance their networks with universities and ventures;
- whether Japanese political and economical structures can be changed from being centrally guided with big businesses to being a market-based decentralized economy relying on local initiatives;
- changes in corporate finance, from debt oriented to debt and equity balanced;
- changes in employment, from lifelong with one chance of recruitment to diverse working styles with a more flexible recruiting system;
- changes to the Bankruptcy Act, from accusation of failure to assistance.

We are progressing rapidly, but there are still many tasks to be solved in Japan.

Notes

1 Roots of the IP drive and economic globalization

1 *Kozo Kaikaku No Shinjitsu: Takenaka Heizo Daijin Nisshi* (The Truth of Structural Reforms: The Diary of Minister Takenaka Heizo), Nihon Keizei Shimbunsha, December 2006.
2 Nagano Satoshi, 'Lessons learnt from non-performing loans to Japan after the 1990's', unpublished paper, 3 September 2006, pp. 1–4.
3 Ibid., pp 4–8.
4 *Kozo Kaikaku No Shinjitsu*.
5 Ruth Taplin (ed.) *Risk Management and Innovation in Japan, Britain and the United States*, Abingdon: Routledge, 2005, and Mr Fukui Toshihiko's interview, taken from 'A talk with Japan's top banker', *Japan Echo* 34(5), October 2007, pp. 45–50.
6 Ruth Taplin organized a seminar at Chatham House with the TSE President, Mr Tsuchiya, speaking to explain for the first time to a London audience the changes occurring at the TSE. Mr Tsuchiya was the first President of the TSE and the first person to travel abroad to explain these changes.
7 Taplin (ed.), *Risk Management and Innovation in Japan, Britain and the United States*.
8 Ruth Taplin, 'Japan's foreign policy towards Southeast Asia', in Richard L. Grant (ed.) *The Process of Japanese Foreign Policy Focus on Asia*, London: The Royal Institute of International Affairs, Chatham House, 1997, pp. 72–107, and Ruth Taplin, 'Japanese measures against IP infringement', *KnowledgeLink, Thomson Scientific*, August 2005.
9 *Kozo Kaikaku No Shinjitsu*.
10 Nariai Osamu, 'The Koizumi record: a five year economic report card', *Japan Echo* 33(5), October 2006, pp. 40–2, and Kuratomi Masatoshi, 'Intellectual property and bridging loans: their emerging roles in venture finance and business rehabilitation in Japan', in Taplin (ed.) *Risk Management and Innovation in Japan, Britain and the United States*, pp. 162–77.

2 Japan as an IP nation

1 Terry Young, 'Technology transfer from US universities: the need to value IP at the point of commercialisation', in Ruth Taplin (ed.) *Valuing Intellectual*

Property in Japan, Britain and the United States, London: RoutledgeCurzon, 2004, pp. 20–33.
2 Nishizawa Akio, 'From tech-transfer to university start-ups: how Japanese universities are responding to new policy change', in Ruth Taplin (ed.) *Exploiting Patent Rights and a New Climate for Innovation in Japan*, London: Intellectual Property Institute, 2003, pp. 39–55. See also Nishizawa Akio, 'Appendix: new challenges for the Japanese universities in the IPR management and spin-off ventures', in Taplin (ed.) *Valuing Intellectual Property in Japan, Britain and the United States*, pp. 146–58.
3 Ruth Taplin, 'Overview: Japanese attitudes to litigation and IPR', in Taplin (ed.) *Exploiting Patent Rights and a New Climate for Innovation in Japan*, pp. 1–7.
4 Ruth Taplin, 'Introduction', in Taplin (ed.) *Valuing Intellectual Property in Japan, Britain and the United States*, pp. 1–20.
5 Quentin Vaile, 'Intellectual property licensing: a history and Japan's continuing corporate advantage', in Taplin (ed.) *Exploiting Patent Rights and a New Climate for Innovation in Japan*, pp. 9–18.
6 Ibid.
7 Ruth Taplin, Appendices 2 and 3, in Taplin (ed.) *Exploiting Patent Rights and a New Climate for Innovation in Japan*, pp. 99–123.
8 *Japan Times*, 24 February 2004.
9 *Kyodo News*, London, 17 May 2007.

3 Historical perspectives of the economy and IP

1 Harald Baum and Takahashi Eiji, 'Commercial and corporate law in Japan: legal and economic development after 1868', in Wilhelm Rohl (ed.) *History of Law in Japan Since 1868*, Leiden: Brill, 2005, pp. 335–6.
2 Ibid.
3 Ruth Taplin, *Decision-making and Japan: A study of corporate Japanese decision-making and its relevance to Western companies*, first published by Japan Library, 1996; reprinted Abingdon: Routledge, 2003, pp. 30–2.
4 Ruth Taplin, 'Overview: Japanese attitudes to litigation and IPR', in Ruth Taplin (ed.) *Exploiting Patent Rights and a New Climate for Innovation in Japan*, London: Intellectual Property Institute, 2003, pp. 1–7.
5 Ibid.
6 Baum and Takahashi, 'Commercial and corporate law in Japan', pp. 344–50.
7 Kuratomi Masatoshi, 'Intellectual property and bridging loans: their emerging roles in venture finance and business rehabilitation in Japan', in Ruth Taplin (ed.) *Risk Management and Innovation in Japan, Britain and the United States*, Abingdon: Routledge, 2005, pp. 162–77.

4 Cross-border IP and the fast-tracking of patent applications

1 Material from the Japan Patent Office (JPO), Tokyo, Japan.
2 'Recent developments at the JPO' by Yamazaki Toshinao, Chief of Europe Section, International Affairs Division, JPO, 19 October 2006, and 'Outline of the bill to Patent Law amendment reducing patent pendency' by Ono Shinjiro,

Deputy Commissioner, JPO, presented at 12th Annual Conference, Fordham University School of Law, 16 April 2004.
3 This material is drawn from an unpublished document prepared by the Japan Patent Office, listing the support the JPO provides for SMEs.
4 'Recent developments at the JPO' by Yamazaki Toshinao.
5 The quotation from Jon Dudas was taken from the USPTO press release no. 08-04, 'USPTO expands patent prosecution highway network to Canadian, Korean patent offices', 28 January 2008.
6 'USPTO and the Japan Patent Office launch electronic priority document exchange', USPTO website, 30 July 2007, nos. 07–28.
7 Information kindly provided by the Administrative Office of the Supreme Court of Japan through Judge Shitara Ryuichi, who created the graphs.
8 'Patently obvious' by Philip Stevens and Paul Howard from the Campaign for Fighting Diseases, 21 April 2008. Also material from the author's own research as a translator of Japanese clinical trial results into English.
9 Adapted from Ruth Taplin, 'Japanese measures against IP infringement in China, South Korea and Taiwan', *Knowledgelink, Thomson Scientific*, August 2005. See also, for the roots of these policies, Arai Hisamitsu, Commissioner of the JPO, 'IPR protection in the 21st century', unpublished paper, 7 May 1997.
10 Ruth Taplin, 'Overview: Japanese attitudes to litigation and IPR' and Appendix, in Ruth Taplin (ed.) *Exploiting Patent Rights and a New Climate for Innovation in Japan*, London: Intellectual Property Institute, 2003; and Ruth Taplin, 'Transforming intellectual property in Japan', *Knowledgelink, Thomson Scientific*, 26 July 2007.
11 'Recent developments in the patent attorney profession in Japan' by Dr Okuyama Shoichi, Okuyama and Co., at the American Intellectual Property Law Association (AIPLA) pre-meeting, New Orleans, January 2007.

5 Changes to the Patent Court and employees' rights to compensation

1 Intellectual Property High Court – booklet issued by the Supreme Court of Japan.
2 Material kindly provided by Judge Shitara Ryuichi, Presiding Judge of the Intellectual Division of the Tokyo District Court.
3 Okuda Hiroshi, Chairman of the Japanese Business Federation, 'Settlement in LED lawsuit could spark surge in lawsuits by inventors', January 2005. Available online at www.asahi.com.
4 Ruth Taplin (ed.) *Exploiting Patent Rights and a New Climate for Innovation in Japan*, London: Intellectual Property Institute, 2003. See also Ruth Taplin, 'Japanese intellectual property and employee rights to compensation', in K. Jackson and P. Debroux (eds) *Asia Pacific Business Review, Special Issue: Innovation in Japan: Emerging Patterns, Enduring Myths*, 14(3), July 2008, pp. 363–79.
5 Material kindly provided by Judge Shitara Ryuichi, Presiding Judge of the Intellectual division of the Tokyo District Court, who presided over the landmark decision in the Nakamura Shuji case.

6 Changes in Japanese corporate governance

1 Ruth Taplin, *Decision-making and Japan: A study of corporate Japanese decision-making and its relevance to Western companies*, first published by Japan Library, 1996; reprinted Abingdon: Routledge, 2003.
2 Takahashi Eiji, 'Japanese corporate groups under the new Legislation', *European Company and Financial Law Review* 3(3), September 2006, pp. 287–310.
3 From *ASBJ Newsletter*, 25 December 2007 (Inaugural Preparatory Issue), pp. 1–12; *ASBJ Newsletter*, 7 July 2008, pp. 1–13.
4 Takahashi Eiji and Shimizu Madoka, 'Does the 2005 reform improve the Japanese economy? The current of Japanese corporate governance reform', in Ruth Taplin (ed.) *The Journal of Interdisciplinary Economics* 17(1/2), 2006, pp. 25–57. (Special issue on international corporate governance, guest editor Takahashi Eiji.)
5 Ibid., pp. 31–3.
6 Takahashi Eiji and Sakamoto Tatsuya, 'Practical experiences with the new Japanese Company Code in 2005/2006', *Journal of Japanese Law* 12(23), 2007, pp. 41–50.
7 Takahashi Eiji and Sakamoto Tatsuya, 'Triangular mergers in Japan', in Kitagawa Zentaro (ed.) *Doing Business in Japan*, Pt VII, Chapter 3, LexisNexus, 2007, pp. 1–22.
8 Ibid.
9 Murakami Hiroshi, '"External" corporate governance: argument about hostile takeover and the poison pill in Japan', in Ruth Taplin (ed.) *Journal of Interdisciplinary Economics* 17(1/2), 2006, pp. 219–47. (A special issue on international corporate governance, guest editor Takahashi Eiji.)

7 Future developments in the Japanese exchanges

1 *Kozo Kaikaku No Shinjitsu: Takenaka Heizo Daijin Nisshi* (The Truth of Structural Reforms: The Diary of Minister Takenaka Heizo), Nihon Keizei Shimbunsha, December 2006.
2 *Innovation Report*, 'Can Europe make it? SME innovation partnering: the missing links' (researched and written by Professor Ruth Taplin, Director, Centre for Japanese and East Asian Studies), PERA, The Innovation Company, 8 November 2005.
3 Ruth Taplin, 'Overview: Japanese attitudes to litigation and IPR', in Ruth Taplin (ed.) *Exploiting Patent Rights and a New Climate for Innovation in Japan*, London: Intellectual Property Institute, 2003, pp. 1–7.
4 Quotation from Mr Saito via the TSE London Representative Office for an article, 'Developments at the Japanese Exchanges', by Ruth Taplin for *Handbook of World Stock, Derivative and Commodity Exchanges 2008*, London: Mondo Visione, pp. lxiii–lxv. Any material used in this chapter from the article is with the permission of Mr Herbie Skeete, publisher, Mondo Visione.
5 See *TSE Mothers Monthly Report*, July 2007. The author thanks the TSE for permission to reproduce this figure and utilize material from the report.

6 Thanks and acknowledgement to Martin Graham, Director of Markets, the London Stock Exchange, for this material.
7 See *TSE Mothers Monthly Report*, July 2007. The author thanks the TSE for permission to utilize material from this report, which is part of a mid-term plan for structural change running until 2010.

8 Conclusion

1 Iwase Tatsuya, 'The government's pension "scam"', *Japan Echo* 34(5), October 2007, pp. 22–3.
2 Leo Lewis, 'Worcestershire Sauce bid gives local flavour to Tokyo downturn', *The Times*, 23 November 2007, p. 69.
3 Takahashi Eiji and SakamotoTatsuya, 'Japanese corporate law: the Bull-Dog Sauce takeover case of 2007', *Journal of Japanese Law* 13(25), 2008, pp. 221–30.
4 Takenaka Harukata, 'Drama in the upper house', *Japan Echo* 35(4), August 2008, pp. 7–9.
5 Shirakawa Hiromichi, 'The Bank of Japan's New Governor', *Japan Echo* 35(4), August 2008, pp. 46–8.
6 Report by the Bank of Japan, August 2008.
7 Kuratomi Masatoshi, 'Intellectual property and bridging loans: their emerging roles in venture finance and business rehabilitation in Japan', in Ruth Taplin (ed.) *Risk Management and Innovation in Japan, Britain and the United States*, Abingdon: Routledge, 2005, pp. 162–77.
8 Press release by the President of the DBJ, 1 October 2008.
9 A number of articles in the October 2008 issue of *Japan Echo* 35(5) reflect issues such as the ageing population, reform of the pension and medical systems, the wrenching changes Japan must make to accommodate the process of globalization, of which Japan is now an integral part, and the importance of Japan's Asian neighbours, especially China.

Index

Abe, Shinzo 40, 94–5
accounting standards 10, 69, 82
Accounting Standards Board of Japan (ASBJ) 10
'Action Plan for the Consolidation of Trading Units' 90
'Advanced Reform Programme' (2001) 4–5
advisory system, courts 59–60
AIM (Alternative Investment Market) 83, 85–6
AIST *see* National Institute of Advanced Industrial Science and Technology
Allotment of Rights without Consideration 98
Alternative Investment Market *see* AIM
Amari Plan 40–1
apparent invalidity defence 58
appraisal rights, shareholders 75
Arai, Hisamitsu 2, 18–19
ASBJ *see* Accounting Standards Board of Japan
ASEAN 12
ASEAN Patent and Trademark Office 23
Asia: economy 11–12, 110; IP infrastructure 106; relations with Japan 23, 106; *see also* China; Korea
Aso, Taro 99–100, 100, 101, 102
Association of South East Asian Nations *see* ASEAN

auditing system reform 70–1, 71–2, 88

banking system 9, 33–4, 36–7; purchase and assumption (P&A) scheme 5; US model 34
Bank of Japan (BOJ) 5, 5–6, 8–9, 9–10, 101, 104–5; *tankan* survey 14–15
bankruptcies 5, 33
'Basic Policies for Macroeconomic Management' (2001) 6
Bayh Dole Act, USA 19
benrishi (patent attorneys) 24, 53–5, 131
boards of directors 71–2, 72, 73; Bull-Dog Sauce 97–8; 'poison pill' 78, 80
Boissonade, Gustav 30
BOJ *see* Bank of Japan
bonds, government 7, 15, 35–6
Bull-Dog Sauce Company 95–9
bushi (knightly nobility) 28–9
business remuneration 21

call options 77–8
capitalism 31
CEFP *see* Council on Economic and Fiscal Policy
China 22, 25, 50–1, 106; cooperation with 11, 12, 51–3
class system 30, 31
Code of Civil Procedure 57, 57–8
collateral, IP as 37–8, 105

Commercial Code 70–1, 72, 77–8, 80
Commercial Code Enforcement Ordinance Act 34–5
Company Code 71–5, 76, 98
company law reform 34–5, 70–4
competitiveness, industrial 109
Consumer Price Index (CPI) 9
consumption tax 1, 13, 15, 103
Copyright Law 61
Corporate Code of Conduct 88
corporate governance: reform 71–4; self-preservation 80
corporate law *see* company law reform
Corporation Law 88
corruption 2
Council on Economic and Fiscal Policy (CEFP) 6–7, 13, 14
counterfeiting, China 51, 52
countervalue (*gappei taika*) 74–5, 76
court system 24–5, 56–8; expert advisers 59–60; protective orders 60–1; *see also* law; litigation
CPI *see* Consumer Price Index
cross-border cooperation 11, 12, 50, 51–3; *see also* intellectual property (IP) highways
cross-shareholding 68–9, 77
currency *see* yen
current value accounting 69
customs, import injunctions 54

daimyo (feudal lords) 28, 29–30
Day of Invention 23
DBJ *see* Development Bank of Japan
debt, corporate 3
delisting criteria, Tokyo Stock Exchange (TSE) 91–2
Democratic Party of Japan (DPJ) 100, 103
Design Law 61
Development Bank of Japan (DBJ) 7, 14, 36–7, 38, 105
Diet, conflict 99–100, 100
directors *see* boards of directors
disclosure, traditional attitudes 5, 9
dividends, shareholders' 73
DPJ *see* Democratic Party of Japan

drug patents 39, 46, 49–50
Dudas, Jon 45

economic crisis, 1990s 3–4
economic/fiscal reform 1–9, 12–16, 111, 114–15
Economist Intelligence Unit IP survey 25–6
Edo period 17, 30, 31
electronics, infringements 50–1
'Emergency Action Programme for Structural Reform' (2001) 5
employees' rights, IP 61–2; Nakamura decision 62–6; Supreme Court judgments 64, 66–7
employment 4–5, 15
endaka (appreciation of yen) 3, 4
English/Japanese feudalism 28–30
European Bank of Reconstruction 105
European Patent Office (EPO) 43–4, 44
exchange companies (*kawase kaisha*) 33
Exchange Law (1893) 36
expert advisory system, courts 59–60

family groups 28
family-owned businesses 68
FDA *see* Food and Drug Administration, USA
FDI *see* foreign direct investment
feudalism, England/Japan 28–30
financial system *see* banking system
floating shares 91
Food and Drug Administration (FDA), USA 49–50
foreign direct investment (FDI) 11, 14, 77, 82; 'poison pill' as barrier to 96, 99
foreign stock companies 74–6; *see also* hostile takeovers
free market economy 7, 27, 104
Free Trade Agreement (FTA), South Korea 12
French legal system 30
Fujitsu 50

Fukuda, Yasuo 94, 95, 99–100, 100
Fukui, Toshihiko 8–9

GAAP (generally accepted accounting principle) 10, 69, 82
gappei taika (countervalue) 74–5, 76
Genji clan 29
German economic model 27
German legal system 30–1
giri (reciprocal obligation) 3
globalization 8, 23; and 'poison pill' 76–80, 96–7; *see also* patent prosecution highways (PPHs)
government bonds 7, 15, 35–6

Hashimoto, Ryutaro 1, 13, 15, 18
Hitachi judgment 64, 66–7
Hokuetsu Paper Company 77
Honda, Soichiro 32
Honda Motor Company 51, 52
hostile takeovers 76–7; 'poison pill' defence 69, 77–80, 95–9
Hyundai 50

IASB *see* International Accounting Standards Board
Ibuka, Masaru 32
IFRS *see* International Financial Reporting Standards
Iijima, Isao 2
imports, customs injunctions 54
incentives for innovation 21
incomes, disparity 15
India 26, 106
inflation rates 104–5
information technology (IT), Tokyo Stock Exchange (TSE) 9, 81, 82
infringement 22, 43; China 50–1; customs procedures 54; Japan/China cooperation 11, 12, 51–3; *see also* litigation
in-licensing 21–2
innovation 17–19, 20, 25–6, 103; incentives for 21; in-licensing 21–2; public involvement 13, 23–4; SMEs 83–4; *see also* employees' rights, IP; universities
Insider Information Centre 92

insider trading 92–3
intellectual property (IP): as collateral 37–8, 105; infrastructure 106; management of 41; public involvement 13, 23–4; valuing 20–1, 37
intellectual property (IP) divisions, universities 19–20, 125–6
Intellectual Property (IP) High Court 24–5, 56–8, 59, 60
intellectual property (IP) highways 10, 39, 106; Korea 11, 43; *see also* patent prosecution highways (PPHs)
intellectual property rights (IPR) 10; Asian cooperation 11, 12; electronics 50–1
International Accounting Standards Board (IASB) 10, 69, 82
International Financial Reporting Standards (IFRS) 69
invalidity defence 58–9
inventions *see* innovation
inventors, neglect of 41
IP *see* intellectual property
IPR *see* intellectual property rights
Ishimaru, Kimio 20
IT, Tokyo Stock Exchange (TSE) 9, 81, 82
Ito, Hirobumi 34

Japanese Financial Services Authority 7
Japanese Institute for Invention and Innovation (JIII) 23–4
Japanese Patent Information Organization (JPIO) 23–4
Japan Highway Public Corporation 6
Japan International Cooperation Agency (JICA) 50
Japan IP Arbitration Centre 54
Japan Patent Attorneys Association (JPAA) 24, 53
Japan Patent Office (JPO) 18, 22, 23, 39–40, 54, 55, 58–9; assistance for SMEs 42–3; *see also* patent prosecution highways (PPHs)

Japan–Singapore Economic Agreement for a New Age Partnership 11
JASDEC Japan Securities Depository Center 90
JICA *see* Japan International Cooperation Agency
JIII *see* Japanese Institute for Invention and Innovation
job creation 4–5
joint stock companies 33, 34, 36
JPAA *see* Japan Patent Attorneys Association
JPIO *see* Japanese Patent Information Organization
JPO *see* Japan Patent Office
J-SOX 86, 87, 89
Justice System Reform Council 56

Kamakura *bakufu* 29
kanji (Chinese characters) 94
Kanto Local Finance Bureau 97
Kato, Taisuke 20–1
katoku (head of *bushi*) 28–9
kawase kaisha (exchange companies) 33
Keidanren 69, 76
keiretsu see sogo shosha/keiretsu
Kilby decision (2000) 58
KIPO *see* Korean Intellectual Property Office
knowledge clusters 130
Koizumi, Junichiro 1–2, 2, 12, 39, 81, 102
Koizumi government 9–10, 18–19, 22–3, 26, 36, 36–7, 40, 41, 53, 77, 105; company law reform 70–4; economic/fiscal reform 1–9, 12–16
kokutai (mystical form of state) 32
Korea 11, 12, 43, 50
Korean Intellectual Property Office (KIPO) 43
Kyoto Action Plan 23

labour costs 15
land tax system 33
language: modernization 70, 82; use of *kanji* 94

law: company law reform 34–5, 70–4; historical legal system 29–31; modern legal system 31–2; patent attorneys 24, 53–5, 131; patent law reform 23–5, 60–1; stock exchanges 36; technical licensing organizations (TLOs) 19–20; *see also* court system; litigation
Law of Exceptional Provisions to the Commercial Code Concerning the Audit of Stock Companies 70–1
LG 50
Liberal Democratic Party (LDP) 1, 2, 76, 95, 99–100, 100, 101
licensing 21–2, 22
licensing remuneration 21
light-emitting diode (LED) judgment 62–6
Limited Liability Company Law 70
liquidity, Mothers listings 89–90
listing system reforms, Tokyo Stock Exchange (TSE) 86–90, 91–2
litigation: cross-border 50, 52–3; invalidity defence 58–9; traditional attitudes to 17–19; *see also* court system; law
London Stock Exchange (LSE) 36; AIM 83, 85–6

M&A *see* mergers and acquisitions
manufacturing companies 4
markets: AIM 83–4, 85–6; free market economy 7, 27, 104; Mothers 83, 84, 86–90, 91
Matsushita, Konosuke 32
Matsushita group 18, 50
Meiji period 31–2, 33–4, 35
menju-fukuhai 31
merchant class 29, 31, 35
merchant houses 33
mergers and acquisitions (M&A) 74–6; *see also* hostile takeovers
Ministry of Education, Sport, Science and Technology (MEXT) 19–20
Mitsui *zaibatsu* 11, 17, 34, 35
Mothers (market of the high-growth and emerging stocks) 83, 84, 86–90, 91

Index 145

moving strike convertible bonds (MSCBs) 87
Munekuni, Yoshihide 51
Murofushi, Minoru 105
Muromachi *bakufu* 29

Nakamura, Shuji 62–6
National Banking Decree (1872) 34
National Centre of Industrial Property Information (NPIT) 42
National Institute of Advanced Industrial Science and Technology (AIST) 20
NEET (not in education, employment or training) population 15
Nichia Corporation 62–6
Nihon Paper Company 77
Nippon Keidanren 69, 76
Nishizawa, Akio 19–20, 107
Nissan 51
nobility (*bushi*) 28–9
non-manufacturing companies 4
non-performing loans (NPLs) 4, 5, 7, 14, 37
NPIT *see* National Centre of Industrial Property Information

obligation, reciprocal (*giri*) 3
ODA *see* Orphan Drug Act, USA
Office for Promotion of Justice Systems Reform 24
offices of first/second filing (OFF/OSF) 44
Oji Paper Company 77
Okuma, Shigenobu 33
Old Commercial Code (1893) 34–5
Olympus v. Tanaka (2004) 64
open licensing policies 21
Orphan Drug Act (ODA), USA 49–50
Osaka High/District Courts 56, 58, 59, 60
oyabun/kobun relationship 29
Ozawa, Ichiro 100, 102–3, 103

P&A *see* purchase and assumption scheme
parent companies 89
Paris Convention for the Protection of Industrial Property 18, 23, 45

part-time workers 15
Patent and Trademark Office, ASEAN 23
patent attorneys (*benrishi*) 24, 53–5, 131
Patent Attorneys Law 24, 54
Patent Courts *see* court system
patent infringement *see* infringement
Patent Law 58–9, 60–1; employees' inventions 64–5
patent law reform 23–5, 60–1
patent offices *see* European Patent Office (EPO); Japan Patent Office (JPO); United Kingdom Patent Office (UKPO); United States Patent and Trademark Office (USPTO)
patent pools 21–2
patent prosecution highways (PPHs) 10, 41, 43–6; drugs 39, 46, 49–50; *see also* intellectual property (IP) highways
patents: as collateral 37–8; validity/invalidity 58–8; world rankings 25–6
patent system 17–18, 32; fast-tracking 39, 39–43, 46, 47–8; globalization 23; *see also* intellectual property (IP) highways
pensions, lost records 94–5, 101
PFIs *see* private finance initiatives
pharmaceutical patents 39, 46, 49–50
'poison pill' defence strategy 69, 77–80, 95–9
political feudalism *see* feudalism
politics: conflict causing stagnation 99–100, 100; future prospects 102–3, 103
population, involvement in IP 13, 23–4
PPHs *see* patent prosecution highways
prices 104–5
prior-art searches 40, 42
priority documents 45
private finance initiatives (PFIs) 8
privatization: Development Bank of Japan (DBJ) 105; public corporations 7

'Promoting University–Industry Technology Transfer' 19
protective order system, courts 60–1
public corporations, privatization 7
public expenditure 7–8, 15
public sector reform 13–14
purchase and assumption (P&A) scheme 5

quantitative easing 8

R&D *see* research and development
racketeers, company (*sokai-ya*) 72
reform: auditing system 70–1, 71–2, 88; company law 34–5, 70–4; economic/fiscal 1–9, 12–16, 111, 114–15; patent law 23–5, 60–1; Tokyo Stock Exchange (TSE) 86–90, 90–1
'Reform and Prospects' 6
'Reform Schedule' 6, 7
research and development (R&D) 25, 37
retirement pensions debacle 94–5, 101
retirement remuneration 73
Ricoh 53
risk: systemic 5; traditional attitudes 82, 101–2

Saito, Atsushi 83
Samsung 50
samurai warrior class 28, 33, 34
sauce company takeovers 95–9
shachokai (meetings of company presidents) 69
shares/shareholders 34, 35, 70–2, 72–3; appraisal rights 75; Bull-Dog Sauce case 97–8; cross-shareholding 68–9, 77; triangular mergers 74–6; Tokyo Stock Exchange (TSE) reforms 91–2; *see also* hostile takeovers
Shimosaka, Sumiko 24, 53–4
shinkabu-yoyakuken (stock acquisition rights) 77–80
Shinohara, Chief Judge 57
Shirakawa, Masaaki 104

Shitara, Ryuichi, Judge 62–3, 65–6
Singapore, trade agreement 11
small and medium-sized enterprises (SMEs) 4, 42–3, 83–4, 105; AIM 83, 85–6
social security system 14
sogo shosha/keiretsu (large conglomerates) 68
sokai-ya (company racketeers) 72
Sony 32
South Korea *see* Korea
special purpose companies (SPCs) 78–9
Special Zones for Structural Reform 14
standards, accounting 10, 69, 82
Steel Partners Japan Fund 96–9
stock acquisition rights (*shinkabu-yoyakuken*) 77–80
stock companies 33, 34, 35, 36; triangular mergers 74–6; *see also* hostile takeovers
stock exchanges 35–6, 81, 82; *see also* London Stock Exchange (LSE); Tokyo Stock Exchange (TSE)
Strategic Council on Intellectual Property 23, 24
Strategic Programme for the Creation, Protection and Exploitation of Intellectual Property 56
Supreme Court judgments, employees' inventions 66–7
Sweden 25
Switzerland 25
systemic risk 5

Takenaka, Heizo 2, 4–5, 6, 11, 81
takeovers *see* hostile takeovers
Tamura, Kotaro 101
tankan survey, BOJ 14–15
taxes: consumption 1, 13, 15, 103; land 33
technical licensing organizations (TLOs) 14, 105, 117–21, TLO law 19–20
technological development 17–18; Tokyo Stock Exchange (TSE) 9, 81, 82

technology transfer 19
temporary workers 15
TLOs *see* technical licensing organizations
Tokugawa *bakufu* 29, 30, 33
Tokyo Agreement 69
Tokyo High/District Courts 24, 56, 58, 60, 65; Nakamura judgment 62–6
Tokyo Stock Exchange (TSE) 9, 36, 81, 82, 92–3, 93; AIM 83, 85–6; delisting criteria 91–2; Mothers 83, 84, 86–90, 91; reform 86–90, 90–1
TOPIX (Tokyo Stock Price Index) 91
Toshiba 20–1, 50
Toyota 52
trademark infringement *see* infringement
Trademark Law 61
trade secrets 60–1
trading units, Tokyo Stock Exchange (TSE) 90
tradition: attitudes to litigation 17–19; attitudes to risk 82, 101–2; dislike of disclosure 5, 9
transfer remuneration 21
triangular mergers 74–6; *see also* hostile takeovers
Trilateral Offices: Kyoto Action Plan 23; *see also* European Patent Office (EPO); Japan Patent Office (JPO); United States Patent and Trademark Office (USPTO)
'trinity reforms' 14
trusts, 'poison pill' 78–9
TSE *see* Tokyo Stock Exchange
Tsuchiya, Mr 9
Tweedie, Sir David 69

UKPO *see* United Kingdom Patent Office
unemployment 4–5, 15
Unfair Competition Prevention Law 54, 61
United Kingdom (UK): AIM 85–6; London Stock Exchange (LSE) 36, 83, 85–6

United Kingdom Patent Office (UKPO) 44–6
United States (USA) 19, 21, 23, 25, 26, 102, 106, 109, 128; banking model 34; Bull-Dog Sauce case 95–9; drugs for neglected diseases 49–50; 'poison pill' 78
United States Patent and Trademark Office (USPTO) 43–5, 45
universities 18–19, 123–4, 128–9, 133; IP divisions 19–20, 125–6; spin-off ventures 122; start-ups 103, 132
university–industry technology transfer 19
USPTO *see* United States Patent and Trademark Office

'vaccine plan' 78–9
validity of patents 58–9
valuation of IP 20–1, 37
vassalage 28–9, 30
vested interests 6, 14

WHO *see* World Health Organization
women, consumption tax protests 1, 13
Worcestershire Sauce *see* Bull-Dog Sauce Company
Working Group on Company Law, Legislative Council 70
World Health Organization (WHO) 49
World Trade Organization (WTO) 11

XBRL accounting tool 87–8

Yamamoto, Yuji 96
yen 33, 101; appreciation of (*endaka*) 3, 4
Yonezawa, Seiji 64
Yoritomo, Minamoto 29
Young, Terry 19

zaibatsu 68; Mitsui 11, 17, 34, 35
zoku-gin 13

eBooks – at www.eBookstore.tandf.co.uk

A library at your fingertips!

eBooks are electronic versions of printed books. You can store them on your PC/laptop or browse them online.

They have advantages for anyone needing rapid access to a wide variety of published, copyright information.

eBooks can help your research by enabling you to bookmark chapters, annotate text and use instant searches to find specific words or phrases. Several eBook files would fit on even a small laptop or PDA.

NEW: Save money by eSubscribing: cheap, online access to any eBook for as long as you need it.

Annual subscription packages

We now offer special low-cost bulk subscriptions to packages of eBooks in certain subject areas. These are available to libraries or to individuals.

For more information please contact webmaster.ebooks@tandf.co.uk

We're continually developing the eBook concept, so keep up to date by visiting the website.

www.eBookstore.tandf.co.uk